AmericanGirl Library

P9-DHI-884

An absolutely indispensable Guide to Life FOR GIRLS!

HELP!

By Nancy Holyoke
Illustrated by Scott Nash

PLEASANT COMPANY

Published by Pleasant Company Publications
For information, address: Book Editor, American Girl,
8400 Fairway Place, P.O. Box 620998, Middleton, WI 53562.

Questions or comments?
Call 1-800-845-0005, visit our Web site at **americangirl.com**,
or write American Girl, P.O. Box 620497, Middleton, WI 53562-0497.

Printed in the United States of America.
04 05 06 07 08 09 KRH 10 9 8 7 6 5 4 3 2 1
Editorial Development by Peggy Ross, Jeanette Wall, and Roberta Johnson
Art Direction by Kym Abrams and Jane S. Varda

Cataloging-in-Publication Data available from the Library of Congress
ISBN 1-58485-966-0

Dear Reader,

Every month, *American Girl* magazine receives over 1,300 letters from girls asking for advice about the problems they face in everyday life. This book is made up of just a few of those letters.

The letters are about friends. They're about families. They're about feelings—fears and frustrations, anger and love.

True friends listen closely and answer honestly, and that's what we've tried to do in this book. We hope you'll find advice that you can use.

We also hope you'll remember the girls you meet here. Why? Because your school is full of girls just like them—and they could use a kind word from a girl just like *you*.

Your friends at *American Girl*

1 Afraid of the Dark

2 Babysitting

4 Boys

6 Brothers & Sisters

10 Bullies

12 Cartwheels

14 Caught Between Friends

16 Chatterbox

17 Cheating

18 Daredevils

19 Divorce

23 Dopey Presents

24 Fat

26 Fickle Friends

27 Fights & Friends

28 Forgiving

29 Foster Kid

30 Grandparents

32 Hair

35 Hogged by a Friend

36 Home Alone

38 Homesick

39 "I'm SO Embarrassed!"

40 Invitations

42 Jealousy

43 Jitters

44 Left Out

45 Looking Dumb

46 Losing a Friend

47 Making a Friend

48 **Mean Friends**

49 Messy

52 **Middle School**

53 **Money**

56 **Moving**

57 **Nail-biting**

58 **New Baby**

59 **Not a Baby Anymore**

60 **Pets**

62 **Picked Last**

63 Picked On

64 **Popularity**

66 **Practicing**

67 **Procrastination**

68 **Racism**

70 **Shopping**

71 **Sore Loser**

72 **Speaking Out**

73 **Spiders**

74 **Stepfamilies**

76 **Teacher's Pet**

77 **Teacher Trouble**

78 **#@!!*&%!!!**

79 **Too Short**

80 **Ugly**

81 **Unwanted Friends**

82 **Working Parents**

84 **"You Throw Like a Girl"**

86 **ZZzzzzzz (bored!)**

90 **More Help!**

Afraid of the Dark

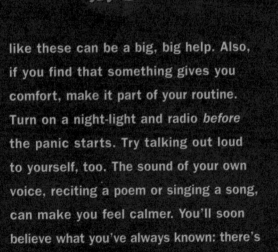

Dear *Help!*,

I'm scared of the dark. I try every-thing in my power not to be. I put the lights on. I listen to the radio. I even go in and sleep with my parents. Sometimes I keep the whole house awake at two in the morning. Help me, please!

Christy

Think: Do you do anything during the day that causes you grief at night? Do you watch scary shows? Do you eat or drink things with a lot of sugar or caffeine after dinner? Changing habits like these can be a big, big help. Also, if you find that something gives you comfort, make it part of your routine. Turn on a night-light and radio *before* the panic starts. Try talking out loud to yourself, too. The sound of your own voice, reciting a poem or singing a song, can make you feel calmer. You'll soon believe what you've always known: there's nothing under your bed but dirty socks.

Babysitting

Dear *Help!,*

My mom just said she is giving me her permission to babysit. She talked to my aunt and told her I would be available. Now what do I do?

Baby Lover

1. Study up.

Spend an evening with your cousins while your aunt is at home. Watch what she does. You'll learn a lot! You might also call your local American Red Cross and ask about babysitting classes. A class can teach you how to take care of babies, handle emergencies, and lots more.

2. Be a businesswoman.

What do other girls your age charge to babysit in your town? Find out, and set your own rates. You might also want to advertise your service to neighbors through flyers or phone calls.

3. Be prompt.

When you land a job, plan ahead about how to get there, and *be on time*.

4. Know the territory.

What are the rules for bedtime? Meals? TV? Where are the diapers and the favorite toys? Ask questions before the parents go, while you have the chance.

5. Write down phone numbers.

Most parents will leave a note about where they're going and include a phone number where they can be reached. If they don't, ask! You should have local emergency numbers, too.

6. Watch the kids, not the TV.

You're there to keep the children safe, and for little kids in particular that means never letting them out of your sight. Ever.

7. Be firm.

When a child throws a tantrum or won't do as he's told, you may fear you can't handle it. You can. You're bigger and wiser than he is (even though it may not feel that way!). Be fair, kind, calm, and patient. But be firm. What you say goes.

8. Get in the spirit.

Really play with the kids. Make them laugh. Make yourself laugh, too! The kids will fuss less, and you'll all have a lot more fun.

Boys

Dear *Help!*,

My best friend means so-o-o much to me! But now that we're getting older, she is getting into boys. It seems like they are more important than I am!

When a good friend goes boy crazy, it can feel like a true betrayal. But the real danger to your friendship isn't that boys will become more important to this girl than you are. (After all, she'll still want girlfriends—to giggle with at sleepovers, to confide in, and more!) The real danger is that the two of you are beginning to have different interests. Your friend may find she has more fun with girls who are "into boys," like she is. *You* may find you have more fun with girls who aren't.

For now, do everything you've always done with your friend. But be sure to keep friendships alive with other girls, too. That way, if you two do grow apart, you'll have somewhere else to turn.

Dear *Help!*,

I told a friend about a boy I like. I thought I could trust her, but the next day everyone in class knew about it.

betrayed

Your friend shouldn't have done this. But the truth is, secrets about boys are the kind almost nobody keeps. They're too much fun to tell. From now on, whenever you open your mouth to tell a friend about a boy you like, picture your secret on the chalkboard. If that doesn't bother you, go ahead and tell. If it does, keep the news to yourself.

Dear *Help!*,

There's this boy at school that I like. He's cute, funny, and nice. But I'm not sure how to tell him that I like him. How can I tell him?

Puzzled

Easy! You don't need to. If there's a girl you really like, do you make a big deal of saying "I like you" to her? Probably not. You talk to her. You sit next to her at lunch. You ask her to do things. That's how one person shows she likes another. Do the same things with this boy. He'll get the message. You'll gain a friend, too.

Brothers & Sisters

Dear *Help!*,

My sister drives me nuts! I need some plan to get back at her. Here are the things she does to me:

1. She puts mayflies in my bed.
2. She puts fake bugs in my slippers.
3. She comes into my room when I tell her not to, and then when I ask her to go away she says, "It's a free country."

I can't talk to her because she'll destroy me before I say a word. Believe me, I've tried!

Caroline

Bad news, Caroline: "getting back" at someone just about never works. If you do something nasty to your sister, next time you'll find *real* bugs in your slippers instead of fake ones.

Try this instead: do something *so* nice for your sister that she won't be able to believe it. She'll go crazy wondering what you're really up to. In the meantime the fighting might die down enough that you two could actually imagine being friends.

Dear *Help!*,

My brother is my best friend, but when he has friends over he acts like I'm not there. Sometimes I go in my room and cry.

Very Hurt!

It sounds as if your brother wants some privacy with his friends. Let him have it, and try to find something fun to do on your own. This can be hard, but not as hard as living with a brother who thinks you're a pest. Guaranteed: he'll be happier to see you at dinner if you haven't followed him around all afternoon.

Brothers & Sisters

Dear *Help!*,

My mom and dad never hear my side of the story when I get into fights with my sisters. Right away it is my fault. Take my word, it is not easy being the oldest.

FED UP

True. It isn't easy. Adults sometimes expect an older kid to be more patient than they are themselves. But the fact is that fighting is a bad way to solve a disagreement. Your parents don't *care* what caused the fight. They're unhappy there was a fight to begin with.

Try this: wait till everyone has cooled down—including you. Then talk to your parents privately. Don't say, "It was all Jenny's fault because she tore my notebook!" In fact, don't say the word "fault" at all. Instead, try to solve the problem. Say, "Jenny comes into my room, even though I tell her not to. Can you help me?"

Then do what they suggest. Your parents will see that you're really *trying* to get along with your sisters. The next time there's trouble, they'll be less quick to come down on *you.*

Dear *Help!*,

My sister pretends she's a cat. She'll answer the phone and say, "Meow?" She's been doing this since February, and I think I'm going to go mad!

Mary

Well, you can't hide her under a bucket, and you can't turn her into somebody else. So look at it this way: no sister is *purr*-fect. At least yours seems friendly, and she's not going to keep this up forever. Every girl wants to be able to express herself—even little sisters. Her family should be the last to tell her she can't.

9

Bullies

Dear *Help!*,

The boy next door always kicks me and pulls my hair. I'm afraid if I fight back, he might hurt me even more. If I tell his parents, he'll get punished, but he'll still beat me up. What should I do?

Scared

Tell. Talk to your own parents first. They can talk to this boy's parents or come with you when you do. This boy is never going to be the ideal neighbor. But if he knows you won't cover up for him, he'll think twice before he hurts you again.

Dear *Help!*,

There are two girls who use me, and it hurts. They ask me for money or something, and say, "Do it or I won't be your friend." I've refused them a few times, and it turned into a war. Usually I give them what they want. I don't know what to do!

Used

What awful girls! There is absolutely no reason you should put up with this. Next time they come around, tell them no. You don't need to be afraid of them. They can call you names. They can yell. They can stomp their feet. But take away their friendship? Hardly! Their friendship is something they've never given you— and judging from their actions, it isn't worth much.

11

Cartwheels

Dear _Help!_,

Whatever I do I cannot turn a cartwheel. I've been trying to learn for about a year. I'm nine, and all my friends can turn one. Even my six-year-old brother can turn one better than I can.

Trying to turn

Then brush up on your handstands. **Practice leaning forward like this, keeping one leg straight.**

Get your body ready.

You'll need strong arms and good flexibility. Ask a Phys. Ed. teacher to recommend exercises that will help you stretch and build strength.

Then kick your legs up into a handstand and hold it, leaning against the wall. Have a parent stand by to help.

Now try a cartwheel. **It's really the same old handstand, only sideways.**

Count 1. **Reach down. Place your hand down sideways instead of straight ahead.**

Count 2. **Kick your feet up over your head, keeping your back straight. Your arms and legs are like the spokes of a big wheel.**

Count 3. **Your first foot touches.**

Count 4. **Your second foot touches. Ta-da! You're done!**

13

Caught Between Friends

Dear *Help!*,

I have two best friends, but they absolutely hate each other! I invited both to my birthday party, and they told each other off. I feel like I'm in a tug-of-war.

Stretched between 2 friends!!

Are these two fighting over you? If so, try to calm their jealousy by telling each one how much you care about her. At the same time, make a few things clear:

(a) You aren't going to drop either friend just because they can't get along.

(b) You'll respect these girls' feelings by spending time with them separately and not playing favorites.

(c) They should respect *your* feelings by not fighting when you're around.

Dear Help!,

I have two friends, Sarah and Elizabeth. I like both of them a lot, but Sarah is always saying mean things about Elizabeth. If I say I don't agree, Sarah might not like me anymore. So usually I say, "I know what you mean."

Perplexed

The next time Sarah makes a mean remark about Elizabeth, tell her flat-out you disagree. If she gets mad, say you don't think a girl should say bad things about a friend behind her back. You wouldn't speak badly of Sarah. And you're not about to speak badly of Elizabeth, either.

Chatterbox

Dear *Help!*,

My best friend and I sit right next to each other, but she talks too much during class. Then we get in trouble. I tell her not to talk to me when we're working, or when the teacher's talking, but she seems to forget.

Worried

Tell your friend you're really worried about this. Let her know that you're absolutely, positively going to stop talking—even if she doesn't. The next time she talks to you in class, don't answer. She can't have a conversation by herself.

If this doesn't work, there's still one thing that will: Speak to your teacher privately and ask him to move you to another seat.

Cheating

Dear *Help!*,

My friend gets good grades. The problem is that to get those good grades, she cheats. I've seen her. I'm afraid to tell the teacher because my friend might dump me, and nobody else will want to be my friend because I'm a tattletale.

Mitfed

Make up your mind to talk to her. Tell this girl straight out that you know what she's doing and it's wrong. Be prepared: she'll probably be mad. Cheaters tell themselves all kinds of lies about why their dishonesty "isn't so bad." But she may also feel ashamed and scared enough to stop—and you won't have had to tell on her to get her to do it.

Daredevils

Dear *Help!*,

Some of my friends are really daring. They ask me to do things that might get me in trouble. I don't want to do them, but I have to, or my friends will call me a chicken.

Cheryl

If you don't want to do something, don't do it. *You're* the best judge of what's right for you. If your friends call you a chicken, ignore them. They're turkeys to bully you.

Divorce

Dear *Help!*,

My parents are getting a divorce. They say everything will stay the same. I know things will change! I like it when they're together. I'm really mad at them. They didn't even think of me!

mad

Things *will* change. You're right. You may not like all the changes, either, and it's natural to be angry about that. But don't think your parents didn't give you a thought. Most parents worry about their kids a lot before divorcing, and do what they do because they truly believe it's for the best. That *doesn't* mean you have to agree with them. And you can tell them honestly just how mad you feel. Just don't retreat into your anger and close the door. Don't lock up your love for them—or lock out their love for you.

Divorce

Dear *Help!*,

My parents just split up. It's hard to tell my friends why my dad's not here. I'm afraid I'll start to cry.

American girl age 10

There's a storm of grief and fear and anger in your chest. You may feel ashamed and embarrassed, too. Talking with a friend can let all these feelings out. Pick a quiet time and place to tell the news to a girl you really care about. And don't be ashamed to cry! You've got a lot to cry about. Afterward, you'll feel less alone, and that will help.

Dear *Help!*,

My parents are divorced. My dad's always saying mean things about my mom and trying to be the best.

Confused

Your dad is wrong to do this. Don't get into an argument about whether what he's saying about your mom is true. Instead, the next time he says something mean about her, tell him his words are hurting you. Tell him you love him, but let him know that if he loves you, he should be more considerate of how you feel.

Dear *Help!*,

My parents are divorced and my dad got transferred to Indiana. Now twice a month I have to go to my dad's. I love my dad, but three hours in a car every other weekend is enough! It's been two years since he moved, and I'm tired of it. I don't want my dad to be sad, but I can't help it. I just don't like that drive.

Torn in Two

Traveling back and forth can be hard—*very*. Next time you visit your dad, talk to him about the problem. Could you go less often but stay a little longer sometimes? Could your dad spend the weekend in your town now and then? Or is there something that would make the car trips more fun—like taking a friend along for the weekend? Think hard, and ask your dad to think with you. See how many ideas you come up with, and then pick one or two to try.

Divorce

Dear *Help!*,

My best friend's parents are separated and will probably get a divorce. She never talks about it at school, but she says she cries herself to sleep every night. What can I do to comfort her?

Omaha Girl

Include your friend in all the fun you can. Right now, her house is clearly a sad place to be. She may be less interested in talking about her troubles than she is in getting away from them.

Of course, if this girl *does* want to talk about her family, you should be ready to listen. Reassure her that it's O.K. to cry. Don't say anything bad about either of her parents. And never, ever repeat anything she says. Do this, and you're a true friend.

If It Happens in Your House:

Over half the marriages in the United States end in divorce. That doesn't mean you have to like it. But it does mean lots of other girls have gone through the same thing. Remember this on days you're dying of sadness. If other girls can survive divorce, you can, too.

Dopey Presents

Dear *Help!,*

Sometimes my parents and grand-parents give me clothing that I really think is dopey and ugly. I don't want to hurt their feelings, so I say I like it. This happens a lot. What should I do?

Rebecca

When you get a gift you don't like, thank the person as warmly as if you did. Later on, gently tell your mom or dad you'd prefer something else and ask if you can exchange it. Most adults don't want to spend money on things a kid really won't use. So be honest, but be polite.

Fat

Dear *Help!*,

I'm always getting teased about my weight. My brother calls me things like Porker and Big Bacon. The worst part is, I can't seem to lose the weight. When kids tease me, I not only feel fat, I feel stupid, because they think I don't know the weight is there. Do you know any ways to lose weight besides dieting?

Too Heavy

Bodies come in all sizes and shapes. Some girls are naturally heavier than others, and are healthy and attractive that way. You need to know what weight is right *for you*. So ask your mom to go with you to a doctor. The three of you can discuss just what to do. Will you need to "go on a diet"? Not exactly. Eating cottage cheese for two weeks isn't going to do you a bit of good. But eating healthy foods all year? And getting some exercise? Now *that* could make all the difference in the world.

Dear *Help!*,

I have a friend, Debbie, who is always saying that she's ugly and fat when she's really not. She's very, very pretty and is very, very slender. I try to tell her but she won't believe me.

Anne in Virginia

Your friend may be putting you on, just pretending to be modest to encourage compliments. Or she may truly lack confidence. But she may also be in the early stages of an eating disorder. This is an illness in which a girl believes she's too heavy and starves herself to the point that it can threaten her life. Think: Does your friend go on extreme diets? Is she moody? Secretive? Does she go overboard on exercise? Have you ever seen her throw up on purpose? Does she spend a lot of time in the bathroom after a meal? If the answer to several of these questions is yes, you or one of your parents should talk to the school nurse. Your friend may need professional help.

Fickle Friends

Dear *Help!*,

I have a good friend in my class—sometimes! One day we're best buddies, but then she doesn't like me anymore. It's like a light switch, on and off, on and off. My other friends say she's using me. What should I do?

Mixed Up

Ask her about it nicely. Say, "Why didn't you talk to me during lunch? Did I do something that made you mad?" If she's really your friend, she must have a reason for "turning off" to you, and she'll tell you what it is. Then you can work things out.

And if she *can't* tell you why she ignores you, or denies that she does? Then the sign reads: B-E-W-A-R-E. She's treating you badly, and she's not being honest. The last thing you want is a friend who hurts your feelings again and again.

Fights & Friends

Dear *Help!*,

My friends and I always get into fights. It happens so suddenly. One person starts ignoring another person, and before we know it we're all in the fight. I hate it. Help!

Kate in Missouri

You can't control all these different friends, but you *can* control yourself. Don't take sides just because sides are forming. Don't fuel the fight by carrying gossip between groups. Be friendly to everybody, and let the storm blow on through.

Forgiving

Dear *Help!*,

My friend's mom was driving in her car with my friend and hit my dog and killed him. I don't want to have to forgive them, and I don't know if I can.

Hurt

When something terrible happens, a person often needs somebody to be mad at. The sadness is so hard to bear! But anger can weigh you down like a two-ton rock. You *need* to forgive your friend and her mom, as much for your sake as for theirs.

Tell your friend you need time to get over your dog's death. If you can't tell her to her face, write a note. You *know* it was an accident. While you grieve for your dog in the days ahead, remind yourself of accidents you yourself have caused and how horrible you felt about them. As you accept your loss, your anger will cool, and with luck forgiveness will follow.

Foster Kid

Dear *Help!*,

I'm a foster child, and I just moved into a new neighborhood. All the kids make fun of me because of my position in life. When I go outside to play they never come over, and they avoid me like I have a disease. How can I show them I'm just like they are?

Disease Girl

No way do you have a disease! It's the other kids who are showing unhealthy signs—of ignorance.

Talk to your foster parents. They know the block better than you do, and may have all sorts of ideas that could help. For starters, perhaps they know which of these kids would respond well to an invitation to do something special with you. If you can make a friend of one girl, she can tell the others that you don't come from another planet.

Grandparents

My grandmother died a few weeks ago. Sometimes I see my mom crying. I loved my grandmother with all my heart. Sometimes I cry too. What can I do to stop thinking about my grandmother?

A sad girl

Do everything you usually do: go to school, participate in activities, see friends. These things will keep you from dwelling too much on your grandmother's death. But at other, quieter times you *will* think of her, and it's right that you do. Your sadness is like a door you have to pass through for your life to return to normal. When it does, the memories that made you cry will bring you happiness instead, and your grandmother will live again, in your heart.

Dear *Help!*,

My grandpa has been sick for two months, and my grandma is staying with us. We love each other, but we just don't get along.

At the End of My Rope

P.S. I tried talking with her. She began to cry and said maybe she should go home.

Ask your mom to be the peacemaker. Make a list of things that cause trouble between you and your grandmother— things like, "She says mean things about my clothes" or "She says I'm rude." Then go through them with your mom one by one. Listen to your mom's ideas about what you can do to make things better. Ask if she'll talk to your grandmother as well. Then work at getting along one day at a time. Walls between people build up little by little—brick by brick. They can come down the same way.

Hair

Dear *Help!*,

My mom is always nagging at me to do something nicer with my hair. I don't know how to do much with my hair. What should I do?

M. Z.

2. **Fancy up your ponytail. Gather the top layer of hair into a small ponytail.**

1. **If you have long hair, move your ponytail to a new spot on your head. Or try more than one ponytail.**

Then gather the next layer of hair and add that to the first. Then gather the rest.

3. Make one long ponytail. Braid it. Twist it into a bun, tuck in the end, and pin it.

5. Make two small braids. Pin them on top of your head with hairpins, tucking in the ends.

4. Or make two ponytails, braid, and do the same thing.

6. Make one small braid by your ear. Wear it straight or pull it over your head like a headband and pin it.

Hair

7. If you have short hair, pull your hair back on one side of your face. Twist it. Then fasten it with a barrette. Wear it that way or do the same thing on the other side, too.

8. Make your own fancy barrettes. Get a variety of ribbon from a fabric store: polka-dot, striped, plaid, plain. Tie the ribbons onto plain metal barrettes.

a.

b.

c.

d.

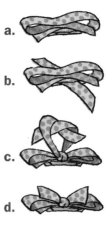

Hogged by a Friend

Dear *Help!*,

I have this friend and she is hogging me. I can't do anything with my other friends unless she's with me.

Hogged

Tell this girl you feel hogged and don't like it. Be kind. Tell her that her friendship is important to you. Tell her that your caring about other girls doesn't mean you care less about her. But let her know you like having lots of friends. If she continues to try to keep you all to herself, she's only going to lose you for good.

Home Alone

Dear *Help!*,

I'm afraid to stay home alone. I'm always thinking a burglar or a murderer will come to my house. When the doorbell rings I'm afraid to open the door. How can I stop being afraid?

Old but Scared

You have a lot of control over how safe you are. The trick is making yourself believe it! There are a number of simple rules that you should follow when you're home alone. A few are listed on the next page. Talk with your parents about others. Type them into a list that you keep near the phone. A stranger at the door or on the phone should be a lot less scary if you know for sure what to do.

Of course it may also be that you're just not ready to stay home alone yet. That's perfectly O.K. Tell your parents how you feel. Together you may be able to figure out another choice.

When you're home alone:

1. Don't answer the door unless you've looked through a peephole or out a window and recognize the person. If it's a stranger, don't open the door. Ever. If there's no way to see who's at the door, keep it shut and call, "Who is it?"

2. Meter readers, repairmen, delivery people—if your parents didn't tell you to expect them, keep the door shut. They can always come back another time.

3. If someone calls and asks for your dad or mom, say that he or she can't come to the phone right now and offer to take a message. Don't say you're alone. If the caller seems too nosy, hang up. Then phone one of your parents and describe the call.

4. Know your neighbors. Keep their numbers next to the phone, along with your parents' work numbers and other emergency numbers. As long as you've got these, you're not totally alone.

Homesick

Dear *Help!*,

I don't like spending the night at friends' houses. I get a funny feeling in my stomach. I can only think about my family and house. Sometimes I go into the bathroom and cry. I end up coming home and feeling confused and humiliated.

Homesick

Don't be ashamed! This is a problem lots of girls have.

If a friend invites you to sleep over, tell her the truth. Explain what it's like for you when you don't sleep at home.

If she's not having a party, maybe you can have her sleep at your house instead. If she is, ask if you can go to the first half of the party and have your parents pick you up before bedtime. You'll still get to share in most of the fun.

"I'm SO Embarrassed!"

Dear *Help!*,

At recess I was doing gymnastics near some boys. While I was landing a handspring, my shirt flew up! The boys began to laugh because I didn't have anything on underneath. Now they won't let me forget it.

Miserable in Virginia

They'll forget it themselves eventually. The joke will get old. They'll tease you less often. They'll discover a new way to get a laugh, and get all caught up in something else. In the meantime, be patient, ignore them, and tuck in your shirt.

Invitations

My birthday is coming up, and I want to have a sleepover. The only problem is, I can only invite five girls. I know who I want to invite, but I don't want to hurt my other friends' feelings. I can only have one party.

Not wanting to hurt

Mail the invitations. Giving them out at school is sure to make the uninvited girls feel worse. You should also be careful not to talk about the party in front of girls who aren't included—and to do what you can to encourage your guests not to talk about it, either. If a girl finds out about the party anyway—as often happens—talk to her. Tell her about the limit your parents set, and ask if she will do something fun with you another time. She'll still feel bad, but she'll also know you're still her friend.

Dear *Help!*,

Every so often a problem comes up. One of my friends calls to see if I can play. Then later a different friend calls to see if I can play. How do I pick who to play with if I know I'll have more fun with the friend who called last?

Mixed Up

If you told the first friend you would go with her, you should do it. Be true to your word.

41

Jealousy

My best friend is good at *everything!* She's so smart. I'm really jealous. She always gets A+'s and special awards, which makes me feel dumb. Whenever I find something I'm good at, she does it five billion times better.

Jealous in Connecticut

The writer William Shakespeare called jealousy "the green-eyed monster," and he had it right. It can really mess up your life if you let it. Already jealousy has made you feel bad about yourself and resent your best friend. And it's done nothing to help you get an A+, either. Drive a stake through its heart! The truth is, everyone has special talents. Don't overlook your own in a desire to have your friend's. If you enjoy something—math, painting, you name it—throw yourself into it with all your heart. You'll discover what fun it is being yourself—and no award can top that.

Jitters

Dear *Help!*,

At school, every year we have tryouts for a play. You have to sing in front of people and dance. I really want to try out, but I'm afraid.

Scared

Practice. Practice alone. Practice in front of a mirror. Practice in front of the dog. Practice in front of your family and your friends. Nothing builds confidence like knowing what you're going to do.

And if you still feel nervous at try-outs? No problem. Nervousness is your body's way of getting you ready for a special event. Nervous energy can turn into creative energy and actually help you do better. When tryouts come, breathe deeply and do your best. If you get a part: great! If you don't, start planning for the next tryout. Sooner or later, you'll land the role you want.

Left Out

Dear *Help!*,

I have two friends. When I'm with one of them everything is O.K. But if the other friend comes over, they always leave me out or gang up on me.

K.* D.*

You've heard it before and it's true: three is often a bad number. Invite your friends over one at a time. Or if the three of you are going somewhere together, bring along a fourth girl or even a fifth. In a bigger group, your two friends will be less likely to pair off. And if they do, you'll still have someone else to be with.

Looking Dumb

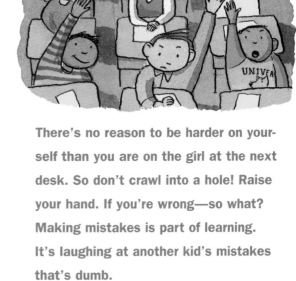

Dear *Help!*,

I'm afraid to answer questions in class. Some kids are really smart and always get the right answers. Sometimes I think the teacher will embarrass me if I say the wrong thing. One time I raised my hand and said the wrong answer, and the boy in front of me snickered.

Embarrassed

There may be *some* kids who always get the right answers, but there must be more who don't. It's not a big deal when somebody else makes a mistake, is it?

There's no reason to be harder on yourself than you are on the girl at the next desk. So don't crawl into a hole! Raise your hand. If you're wrong—so what? Making mistakes is part of learning. It's laughing at another kid's mistakes that's dumb.

Losing a Friend

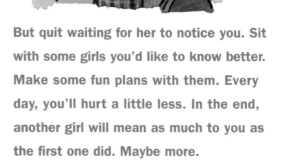

Dear *Help!*,

I have a best friend who now sits with the popular girls. I try my hardest to have her notice me, but she ignores me. I have been best friends with her for a long time. What should I do?

Happy before, not anymore

When a girl ignores you again and again, she's telling you she doesn't want to be friends anymore. It can break your heart, but there isn't much you can do about it except find some new friends. Don't say anything angry to this girl. Be as polite to her as you would be to anyone else.

But quit waiting for her to notice you. Sit with some girls you'd like to know better. Make some fun plans with them. Every day, you'll hurt a little less. In the end, another girl will mean as much to you as the first one did. Maybe more.

Making a Friend

Dear *Help!*,

There's this girl in some of my sixth-grade classes, and she never talks to anyone. She looks very nice, and I would like to make friends with her. My only problem is, how do I introduce myself and not feel like a nerd? And how can I get her to like me?

Jennifer

Relax! There's nothing nerdy about being friendly. Work up your courage and say, "Hi! I'm Jennifer." Ask some friendly questions. This girl sounds shy and you do, too. The two of you may feel awkward at first, trying to find things to say. *That's really O.K.* The important thing is that you were friendly to begin with. Just don't make the mistake of trying to impress her by talking big. Be yourself, and she'll like you fine.

Mean Friends

Dear *Help!*,

I have a friend who is not nice to me at all. She always gets mad if I don't do what she wants. And she talks about me. She will say bad things, then say, "Just kidding!" I get so mad at her!

Katie

You're right to be mad! Don't be a doormat for a friend who treats you poorly. Tell this girl how you feel. If she wants your friendship, she's got to treat you with respect. Tell her you'll walk away the next time she acts badly—and then

do it, even if it's very hard. She'll learn you mean what you say.

Messy

Dear *Help!*,

I just can't keep my room clean. I try and try. Every time I clean it, it gets even messier. I do not like to live in a room where there isn't enough room to walk.

The Messiest Person in Seattle

Less stuff means less mess. Get some grocery bags. Mark them "Give Away," "Garbage," "Basement," "Garage Sale," and so on. Now march over to that closet. Pull things out one by one. Be honest with yourself. If you don't wear it, put it in a bag. If you don't play with it, put it in a bag. If it could be stored in another room—*boom.* Into a bag. Put on some music and sing out loud while you work. Sort the things in the rest of your room, too. The more stuff you put into the bags and get out of there, the better.

HELP!

Then...

Clip barrettes on a ribbon.
One yardstick, six clothespins, a little glue, and some paint makes a hat tree.
Shoe boxes stack!
LETTERS
OLD TAPES
ROCK COLLECTION
Shoe holder and drawstring bag can hold toys, socks, or underwear.
DIRTY CLOTHES
You need this!
WHATEVER
Get them off the bed!
for things that don't go anywhere else

Middle School

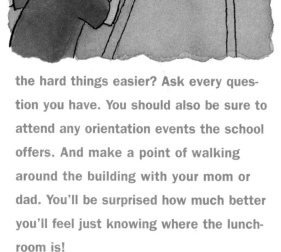

Dear *Help!*,

This year I'll be going to middle school. I don't know what to think. I'm always looking forward to new adventures, but I'm scared at the same time. I mean, what about the older kids and showers and locker combinations. I don't know . . .

Lindsay

You're not alone. Chances are, every kid in your class feels a lot like you. Do this: Talk to some girls who started middle school last year. What was fun about it? What was hard? What would have made the hard things easier? Ask every question you have. You should also be sure to attend any orientation events the school offers. And make a point of walking around the building with your mom or dad. You'll be surprised how much better you'll feel just knowing where the lunchroom is!

Money

Dear *Help!*,

Whenever I get money, I spend it on things I don't really want or need—even though I meant to save for something I really did want. Please help me think of a way to save money.

Wanting to Save

1. Get two cans. Mark them "Save" and "Spend." When you get your allowance or are paid for a job you've done, divide the money equally between the cans. You can take money out of the "Save" can just four times a year. No cheating!

2. Don't take money with you to the mall. If you don't have it with you, you can't spend it.

3. When you spend money on candy and little stuff, save the wrappers. Collect them in a clear jar. It will remind you of just where all that money has gone—and how little you got for it.

Money

Dear *Help!*,

My mother started a business, and now we never have any extra money. She says it takes a while for a business to start, but she's been saying that for the last year! All my friends have money for roller-skating and stuff on weekends. I feel left out.

Nicole

Well, you can't wish away your mom's business. Instead, try thinking up fun things to do with your friends that don't cost money. You can also earn the money you want by starting a business of your own. Many girls babysit, of course. But you could sell things or run errands—there are lots of possibilities. You'll find it feels good to have money you earned yourself—which is probably why your mom started that business in the first place!

ODD JOBS
RAKING ★ FIX-IT
SWEEPING &
CLEANING &
MORE!

RED FLYER

Things you can sell—**Start with neck-laces you've beaded yourself.** ✦ **Or buy a variety of ribbons at a fabric store, cut them into lengths, put several colors together in a packet, and sell them to girls to wear in their hair.** ✦ **Have a one-girl garage sale and sell old toys.** ✦ **Sell popcorn at soccer games, apples at football games, homemade lemonade at swim meets.** ✦ **String cranberries and popcorn, and sell the strands as decora-tions at Christmas.** ✦ **Always charge more than your materials cost you, but not a lot more.** ✦

Services you can offer to friends and neighbors—**Mow lawns, weed gardens, rake leaves, shovel snow.** ✦ **Walk dogs. Wash dogs.** ✦ **Wash cars and windows.** ✦ **Help with recycling.** ✦ **Do dusting.** ✦ **Take in mail, water plants, and care for animals while people are on vacation.** ✦ **Run errands on your bike.** ✦ **Tutor.** ✦ **Start a playgroup with a friend where parents can leave toddlers for a few hours each week.** ✦ **Make treasure hunts for kids' parties.** ✦ **Make a haunted house and charge admission.** ✦ **Wrap your head in a towel and tell funny fortunes.** ✦

Moving

Dear *Help!*,

My parents want to move and I truly don't. I don't want to leave my friends or my school. I am scared to death about it.

Against the moving trucks

Saying good-bye is a lot easier if you've arranged a time to say hello again. If you aren't moving far, plan a return visit. If you are, promise your friends that you'll write and call—and then do it.

You might also spend some time before you leave thinking about your life in your new home: How are you going to decorate your new room? What clubs are you going to join at school? What places do you want to visit after you move? Make all the plans you can. You'll dread the move less if you have things to look forward to. And with projects to do and places to go, you'll feel more at home when you get to the new house.

Nail-biting

Dear *Help!*,

I have a bad habit. I bite my nails. I've tried to stop but nothing helps. Everybody else has pretty nails, but mine are little tiny things.

Mad at myself

1. Most drugstores sell a product for girls like you. It's like nail polish, only the taste is horrible. Use it daily. And *keep* using it as your nails begin to grow.

2. Wear gloves while you're watching TV, reading, or hanging out at home. It may look goofy, but it will help.

3. Ask your mom or dad if they'll treat you to a manicure at a hair salon if you don't bite your nails for a week. You'll enjoy working toward a reward, and once your nails are pretty you'll want to keep them that way.

4. Remember, a habit like this is hard to break, so don't let setbacks stop you. If you bite new nails, start over. Your determination will make you succeed.

New Baby

Dear *Help!*,

Ever since my mom had a baby, my parents have ignored me. They only notice me when they tell me to do something. I'm always helping out with the baby and around the house.

Invisible child

What you need are "chore chats." If you're folding laundry with your dad, fill him in on your friends while you do it. If you're drying dishes while mom feeds the baby, tell her about your music class while you work. Your parents love you as much as they always have. They just don't have time to show it. Life will get easier as the baby gets older. But for now you have a better chance of getting their attention if you don't compete with the baby. They'll enjoy your talks and be grateful for your help. Who knows? They may even find a quiet moment to say so.

Not a Baby Anymore

Dear *Help!,*

My mother is turning into my jailer. I don't think she knows she's got to let go of me sometime. I'm just about going insane! For heaven's sake, I'm ten already! She's not letting me grow up!

Mad at Mom

You can't change your mom's opinions about what's safe or what's appropriate for girls your age. (And the fights will only get bigger if you try.) What you *can* do is show your mom you're mature and responsible—about chores, about homework, even about these disagreements themselves. Remember, nothing makes you *look* more like a baby than stomping and yelling. So when your mom says no, stay calm and listen. You'll be a lot more successful in explaining why you think as you do. Chances are, she won't change her mind, but she'll be impressed by your behavior—and eventually that will help.

59

Pets

Dear *Help!*,

I really want another pet, other than what I have now—a rabbit. What I really want is a dog, but I'd be happy with even a little goldfish. Anything but a rabbit that doesn't do anything but just sit there and sniff at you. My parents don't think I'm responsible. I'm plenty responsible!

Doggone!

Hmm. It's clear you've got to prove yourself to your parents. Try this: spend at least two months taking very good care of that rabbit. Feed it, give it fresh water, keep the cage clean. Do all this (a) without complaining, (b) without being nagged, and (c) without asking for a different pet. These actions will show far better than words just how responsible you are. Then try asking again. You may be happily surprised.

Dear *Help!*,

We got a new puppy about a month ago, and my parents are ready to sell him already! Just because he jumps all over us and digs up the flowers and chases the car up and out of the driveway doesn't mean we should sell him *already*.

Desperate

Your puppy's being a puppy! He can't behave like a full-grown dog any more than your two-year-old sister can behave like a grownup. Here's your best hope: Tell your parents that if they'll give the puppy time to grow up and settle down, you'll give him the other thing he needs: training. Your puppy's vet can offer advice on dog-training. A library will have books on it, too. Work with your puppy every day. He'll soon learn the rules.

Picked Last

Dear *Help!*,

In sports I always get picked last because people think I'm slow and can't do anything. I may not be quick, but I have skills! The others put me in places where I don't get to do anything.

Ashley

Being picked last can make you feel as if somebody's hung a sign around your neck that says you're no good. But you're right to say speed isn't everything. Skill in sports is a combination of practice, coordination, and attitude. If you practice and play hard, you should do well. Don't worry for now about what position you play. Just play it as well as you can, and eventually kids may notice you're better than they thought.

Picked On

Dear *Help!*,

All the kids pick on me because I'm different. They say I have cooties and call me names. I keep getting the same advice: "Just ignore it." "Laugh and pretend it's funny." Can you give me different advice?

Not Laughing

You can talk to some of these kids individually, and tell them what they know in their hearts—that what they're doing is wrong and cruel. You can also talk to your teacher and your parents. With teasing this mean, an adult should get involved and call a halt. Above all, don't let these kids make you feel bad about yourself. Look them in the eye! A lot of creative, talented people were picked on for being "different" when they were kids. Besides, your differences express who you are. And it's the girls who are true to themselves who will be the happiest in the end.

Popularity

Dear *Help!*,

I don't need to be really popular. Then again, I don't want to be a down-in-the-dirt nobody, either. What do I do?

Heather

Look into your heart. Who are the girls who make you feel happy to be yourself? Who are the girls who treat you with kindness and respect? Who are the girls who don't change friends every minute? Who are the girls you can trust?

Got the answer? *These* are your friends. Be true to them. They may be "popular" or they may be "nobodies." What other kids think of them doesn't matter a smidge. Neither does what other kids think of *you* for being their friend.

Dear *Help!*,

There is an "in crowd" at our school. They think they are better than everyone else and put other people down. My friends and I try to be friends with them, but every time we try, they either tease us or ignore us.

Teased in Tennessee

Why are you trying to be friends with these girls? They don't sound nice, and it's clear they make you feel crummy. Forget them. If they want to amuse themselves by being mean—that's their choice. But don't set yourself up for a snub.

Practicing

I play the violin. I really like it, but I hate practicing. I don't want to quit. What should I do?

Jessica

Practicing is always easier if you're working toward a goal, like a recital. Try giving a monthly concert for your family. Or find an opportunity to listen to a violinist a level above you and decide you're going to learn to play a certain piece as well as she does. Talk to your teacher, too, about setting other goals, or learning pieces you particularly like.

All these things will help. The truth is, though, that learning *can* be frustrating—and practicing *isn't* always going to be fun. But it is rewarding. VERY. Your instincts are right. Stick with it. You will absolutely, positively be glad you did.

Procrastination

Dear *Help!*,

I have a project I'm supposed to be finishing, but I've hardly started. My mom says my problem is procrastination, or putting things off till later. I've tried writing calendars and schedules, but it doesn't work.

Hopeless

You don't need a calendar. You just need to sit down and start on that project—*now!* And here's an idea that will make you do it: Ask your parents to put your allowance into quarters. For every hour you procrastinate instead of doing your project, they should put a quarter into a jar marked "I'LL DO IT LATER." Once a quarter goes into the jar, you can't have it till your project's done.

Racism

Dear *Help!*,

I'm eleven years old. I am Korean. Boys at school make fun of me because I'm Oriental. Next time they make fun of me, what should I say? If I tell the teacher, they'll make fun of me because I told on them.

It's not easy to stand up to people like this, so it's important that you ask your parents and your teacher for help. Racist teasing is very, very serious. It's serious because it's so hurtful to kids like you. It's serious because it poisons the whole school by allowing kids to imagine racism has a place there. It shouldn't be ignored or tolerated—ever. Therefore:

1. Try to be brave and speak out. When one of the boys makes a nasty comment about your race, say, "That's a racist thing to say." Your friends should speak out, too. This may make him see his "joke" in a very different light. He may feel ashamed and stop.

2. Tell your parents and your teacher what's going on. *This is not a problem that you should have to handle alone.* The adults are in a better position than you are to stop these boys, and it's in the best interest of every child in your school that they do it.

3. Your parents and your teacher will probably talk to the boys and the boys' parents, and that's good. They may also re-examine whether kids at your school are learning enough about the history of racism and cultures different from their own. Remember, this is a complicated problem that people in this country have been fighting throughout our history. Solutions are difficult, and don't happen overnight.

4. A lot of people—children and grownups alike—are afraid to talk about race. They keep their thoughts and feelings hidden under a rock of silence. Don't be one of them! Try to be open about what you see and how you feel, even though that can be hard. Your honesty can get others talking. You'll be doing something important in the fight against racism— and that will feel good.

Shopping

Dear *Help!*,

Here's my problem: my mother picks out my clothes when we go shopping, and she and I have totally different taste in clothes.

Soured on Shopping

If your mom picks out an outfit you really hate, explain nicely what you don't like about it. Then listen to her explain what she does. Is there something else on the racks that will satisfy you both? Or would she pick four or five outfits, and then let you choose among them? If you want one thing badly, you can ask to pay for it with your own money. But don't get hung up arguing about an outfit your mom just plain hates. Compromise. If you don't dig in *your* heels, maybe she won't dig in *hers*, and you'll be a lot more likely to leave happy with what's in the bag.

Sore Loser

Dear *Help!*,

I'm a sore loser. I cry when I lose. I try to hold it in, but I can't!

Annie

Nobody likes to lose, but learning to do it gracefully makes things a whole lot easier. Luckily, you know what's right: you *want* to be a good sport. That desire will soon grow into the self-control you need. For now, if you've got to cry, do it as quickly and privately as you can. Just be sure that when the tears stop, you congratulate the winner as nicely as you would want someone to congratulate you.

Speaking Out

Dear *Help!*,

I know a girl who is always teased. I laugh with everybody else, but I feel so bad! This girl has been teased all her life, and she laughs with people too, even though she must feel bad down in her heart. What should I do to help her?

Sorry and Last

You've probably read books where girls do heroic things like saving someone's life. And you may have wondered what it would be like to be brave like that. Well, here's your chance. Don't go along with the crowd. Tell the teasers that what they're doing is cruel. They may fight back by saying mean things to you. But it will be harder for them next time to pretend this is just a game. You'll need courage to speak out. You'll like yourself, though, if you do. And to at least one girl at school, you'll be a hero in real life.

Spiders

Dear *Help!*,

This might sound silly, but I'm scared of spiders. My mom says just kill them. But spiders look scary!

Audry

True. But think: You are 150 times taller than most spiders. You weigh 10,000 times as much. You're also smarter. It's not much of a contest. Keep that in mind the next time you see a spider skitter across a wall. Don't jump up shrieking. Make yourself move slowly. Keep your voice soft. If you *act* calm, it can help you *feel* calm.

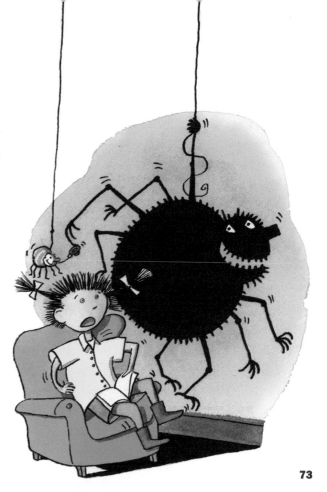

Stepfamilies

My mom got remarried in July. It seems like she cares more for my stepfather and his kids than she does for me and my sisters.

Depressed

Your mom doesn't love them more than she loves you. It just feels that way because you have to share her. Right now, everyone is having to make changes and settle into new relationships. This is all part of what happens when parents remarry and two different families come together. It's natural to feel uncertain and jealous—even angry—at a time like this. The important thing is to talk to your mom about how you feel. That way, she can try to help.

Dear *Help!*,

My dad always brings his new wife to my swim meets even though I tell him that I don't want her there. I don't like her because she was the cause of my parents' divorce. I think she's only pretending to be nice. Should I get revenge or just ignore them?

Mad In Michigan

Neither. By bringing his new wife to your meets, your dad is telling you he's not going to let you ignore her. If you try to "get revenge" by insulting your stepmother or hurting her feelings, you'll damage your relationship with your dad. You'll also damage yourself, by teaching yourself to say and do mean things. You are mistress of your own heart, and nobody can make you like your stepmother, or even forgive her. But don't give hate a permanent home in your heart. If you turn this relationship into a war, the person hurt worst will be you.

Teacher's Pet

Dear *Help!*,

I have always made straight A's. Everyone calls me a goody-goody or teacher's pet. I just try to do my best, but they make it seem like it's bad.

Perfect

Teasing like this often comes from jealousy. Being good in school is something to be very, very proud of. In the bottom of their hearts, the kids who pester you know that. Ask a friend if there's anything you do that makes the others think you're a show-off. If there is, change it. But never, ever play dumb when you're not.

Teacher Trouble

Dear *Help!*,

My teacher is so strict! She never smiles. She reminds me of a rain cloud. She gives out checks if you make one itsy bitsy teeny weeny mistake.

Girl who needs a new teacher

Never smiles? Yikes! Well, study hard, do your homework, and whenever you finish a paper or a test, read it over before you hand it in. This will cut down on little mistakes. You'll also know you've done your best, and that's all any teacher can ask.

At the same time, keep an open mind, if you can. This teacher could surprise you and turn out to be less crabby than she seems right now.

#@!!*&%!!!

Dear *Help!*,

I have a horrible temper. A day doesn't pass without me yelling at my parents or my little brother. I always wish that I could take back everything I said.

frustrated with myself

If you can't control your emotions, practice controlling your body instead. When you feel yourself beginning to blow, say "I have to be alone" and leave the room. Just start walking and don't stop. March up and down a hallway. Stomp around the basement. Go outside and walk around the house. Talk out loud. Do anything that helps you let off steam. You'll cool down eventually. Then if you want to take back something you said . . . do.

Too Short

Dear *Help!*,

I'm in desperate need of advice. I am eleven years old. So what? I am four feet three inches and wear a size one shoe, that's what! I am being teased every minute of my life. If it's not one person, it's another. I'm starting to get very frustrated.

Small in San Jose

P.S. I tried to talk to my teachers. They said, "You know, you guys have to work that out." Well, no kidding.

There isn't a thing in the world wrong with being short. Don't let anyone make you think there is. Here's a ditty that will remind you of that—and put the teasers in their place:

My hands are little,
my skirt petite,
I wear teeny shoes
on tiny feet,
But nothing about me
is quite as small
As a kid who has
no manners at all.

Ugly

Dear *Help!*,

Some days I look really ugly. My friends and I all think so. I know beauty is in the eyes of the beholder, but I still want to be prettier!

Dog face

Prettiness has less to do with a person's features (stuff like the size of your nose and the shape of your eyes) than you might think. What really matters is a healthy look, cleanliness, personal style—and personality. If you really believe in yourself, and beam confidence in your eyes and smile, you're attractive whether you're a beauty or not. So take care of your skin. Wash your hair. But don't, *don't,* DON'T spend time looking in the mirror, searching your face for mistakes. Go do something that makes you happy. Your face will shine with its own light.

Unwanted Friends

Dear *Help!*,

I have a big little problem, and its name is Barbara. She really wants to be my friend. But I don't want to be her friend. No matter where I go she finds me. What should I do?

Frustrated

What you shouldn't do is say: "I don't want to be your friend." After all, there's no reason to be *un*friendly to someone who's friendly to you. You simply don't want Barbara to stick to you like glue. So tell her it seems as if she's following you around. As kindly as you can, say you feel you have no privacy with your other friends. Then be patient. Try to remember that though your situation is tough, Barbara's is worse. She won't keep this up forever. Sooner or later, she'll give up hope and offer her friendship to someone who is glad to have it.

Working Parents

Dear *Help!*,

My mom has been looking for a job, and it seems she may have found one. If she really gets the job, there will be a lot of changes to be made. I'm not sure I'm ready for them!

Unsure

Families grow and change over time, just like the people in them. Right now, you may be worried about what you will do after school or about your new responsibilities around the house. That's natural, and you should talk about these things with your parents, so they can help. Remember, though, your mom's going to work is one more stage in your family's life—like the day you started kindergarten or the day your sister left for college. What seems scary and difficult today will be routine tomorrow.

Dear *Help!*,

My dad works a lot, so my mom and my sister and I hardly ever see him. We all miss spending time together.

Troubled Girl

Say so. Tell your parents you'd like to have an official Family Huddle every week. A Family Huddle is anything that brings all of you together to have fun and talk. One week it could be doing a jigsaw puzzle. The next week it could be taking a walk after dinner. The important thing is that everyone knows when Family Huddle will be and plans for it.

"You Throw Like a Girl"

My teacher is very sexist against girls. Just today, he said to a girl named Catherine after she threw the football, "You throw like a girl." I said, "*What*?" And he said, "Oh, our little women's rights movement person is back there." You know, and so do I, that you can't talk back to teachers, but what do I do?

Elizabeth

Talk to your parents. Ask if they will come with you to talk to the teacher. They can say to him what seems obvious to you: "A bad throw is not the same thing as a girls' throw. It's insulting to girls to say that it is." Your parents may want to talk to the principal, too. In the meantime, don't let this man change how you play sports or think about yourself. Not one teeny tiny bit.

Dear *Help!*,

I'm the only girl on my basketball team. I'm pretty good at it, too. But the boys never pass me the ball.

Amy in Alabama

It's your coach's job to make sure the team plays as a team. Talk to her. If the boys are hogging the ball, she can tell them they're not allowed to take a shot until they've passed at least once to you. She can also put you into some special plays. Either way, you'll be able to show what you can do. If the boys want to win, they'll learn to let go of the ball.

ZZZZzzzz (bored!)

Dear *Help!*,

I stay home alone during summer weekdays. I've done everything to keep myself occupied, but it's no use. I'm so-o-o bored. Y'all got any advice?

An extremely bored Texan

1. Don't assume you're stuck in the house because your parents can't drive you places. See what activities your friends and neighbors are signing up for. Maybe you can sign up, too, and hitch a ride. **2.** Think: what else interests you? Gymnastics? Science? Earning money? Set yourself a goal and work at home to

achieve it. Don't forget about volunteering, either. Look around: whom can you help? **3.** There's nothing worse than eating breakfast with an empty day staring you in the face. Plan ahead. Call friends in advance. **4.** Don't wait for something interesting to happen to you. MAKE it happen. You've got a brain that can think up new twists on old games. You've got a fun spirit waiting to throw off the gloom. Put them to work! The truth is, life is full of problems—boredom's just one of them. Learn to find happiness in little things. It's like spinning straw into gold.

Spinning straw into gold—**Paint a friend's toenails at the same time she paints yours.** ✶ Pretend you moved to Mars. Draw a picture of what your bedroom looks like. ✶ **Do the limbo with a friend under the stream of water from a garden hose.** ✶ **Read every book your favorite author ever wrote.** ✶ **Throw a birthday party for a pet.** ✶ **Do a jigsaw puzzle on the porch.** ✶ **Do a favor for a friend.** ✶ Make a frappé. Put in a blender: 1 cup of fresh or frozen strawberries, 2 tablespoons sugar, 1 cup crushed ice, and 1 cup milk. Mix it up. Mmm! ✶

Draw a picture of your brother with your feet. ⭐ Cook dinner. Play mood music. Be a waiter: take orders. Accept tips. ⭐ Shoot Ping-Pong balls off soda bottles with a squirt gun. ⭐ Wake up at dawn, make cinnamon toast, and watch the sun rise. ⭐ Be fruity. Mold banana beads out of Sculpey clay. Make a banana bracelet. ⭐ Use gel to give your friend a hairdo from outer space. Have her give you one, too. Run through the sprinkler till it's all washed out. ⭐ Be a soccer star next fall: work on your skills by kicking a soccer ball in and out of a line of tin cans. ⭐

Sneak a candy into a friend's pocket. Let her wonder where it came from. ⭐ Dress up. Pretend you're giving a concert while you practice your instrument. Get up now and then to take a bow. ⭐ Start a journal. ⭐ Have a tournament: invite the neighbors to play badminton, croquet, jacks, jump-rope, or charades. ⭐ Write a letter to your grandparents. Put on lipstick and seal it with a kiss. ⭐ Lie down on the driveway. Have someone trace around you with chalk. Draw yourself some clothes and a new hairdo. ⭐ Take the dog for the best walk it's ever had.

Wear sunglasses. Act famous. ✦ Put a picnic cloth on the floor of your room and invite a friend for lunch on a rainy day. ✦ Teach your little brother to dance. ✦ Shoot baskets. ✦ Identify all the trees on your block. ✦ Rearrange the furniture in your room. ✦ Make the world's longest clover chain. Have your mom wear it at dinner. ✦ Get together with your friends for Hawaii Day at the local pool. Hula off the diving board. Wear leis. Drink pineapple juice. ✦ Go for a walk in the rain. ✦ Make a timeline of your life. Put a big fat star on today. ✦

More Help!

You don't have to face your troubles alone. If you need more advice than we've offered here, look around you. Help is there: at home, at school, in the library, at your church or synagogue, in the community.

Talk to your parents. Talk to a teacher. Talk to a counselor at school. Talk to another adult who is close to your family. These people can't solve the problem *for* you, but they can be a big help. If your problem is really serious, an adult can even bring in a professional whose job consists of helping people like you.

Keep in mind that a big problem can't be solved overnight. It's going to take time. If one thing doesn't work, try another. And if *that* doesn't work, try something else. Never, ever give up.

and now, even MORE

HELP!

AmericanGirl Library®

MORE HELP!

By Nancy Holyoke
Illustrated by Scott Nash

PLEASANT COMPANY

Dear Reader,

American Girl magazine gets more than 300 letters a week from girls all over the country asking for advice. A year ago, we collected some of these letters into a book called *Help!* Readers liked it so much we decided to do it again. And so . . . here's *More Help!*

Each girl you'll meet here sat down to write with a troubled heart. The letters are full of feelings—hurt and anger, doubt and sadness. Feelings all girls share.

Will you find advice you can use? We hope so. We also hope you'll remember these girls the next time you see someone at your own school who needs a helping hand—and give her yours.

Your friends at *American Girl*

1 Aargh!
2 Adopted
3 Bad Influence
4 Best Friends
6 Blabbermouth
7 Blushing
8 Bossy
9 Boys
12 Bras
13 Brothers & Sisters
17 Camp
18 Class Clown
19 Clothes
20 Competing
22 Copycat
23 Crybaby
24 Disabled
25 Divorce

29 Fame
30 Fear
32 Freckles
33 Friendless
34 Frustrating Friends
36 Gangs
37 Gossip
38 Grades
39 Gross
40 Haircut
41 Home-schooled
42 Homework
44 "I Hate My Name"
45 Klutz
46 Left Out
47 Lies
48 Locker Room
49 Mooch

50 Movies

51 Munching

52 New Glasses

53 Old Car

54 Only Child

55 Partners

56 Peer Pressure

57 Pentecostal

58 Pets

60 Piano Lessons

61 Picky Parent

62 Pink

63 Popularity

64 Race

67 Roller Coaster

68 Second Choice

69 Sharing a Room

70 Sleepovers

72 Smart

73 Smelly

74 Sports

76 Stepfamilies

78 Teased

79 Teddy Bear

80 Too Busy

81 Too Tall

82 Trying to Be Brave

83 Trying to Be Nice

84 Uninvited Guest

85 Unloved

86 Worrywart

87 the real YOU

88 Zilch

90 Even More Help!

Aargh!

Dear *Help!*,

I have trouble doing things that my mom tells me to do, like:

      (1) shower

      (2) make my bed

      (3) be nice to my sister

      (4) get straight A's.

Aargh! I need help!!!

Crazed in California

When you walk, you put one foot in front of the other. Each step takes you about a foot. Twelve inches may not seem like much, but a girl can get anywhere that way. Remember this when Mom's expectations seem out of reach and you're feeling crazed and hopeless. Pick ONE problem—say, organizing your time in the mornings. Shut out all the rest. Think the problem through and come up with a couple things you can do that might help. Make them your assignment for the week. You'll make a little progress and feel a little better. In other words, if you can't do it all, do what you can. You'll be amazed how far a girl can get chugging along step by step. By step.

Adopted

I am adopted. I told my friend Sally, and she told the biggest gossip in the school. Now everyone knows, and they are asking me questions. What should I do?

a different girl

Kids who don't know anything about adoption are often curious about it, and that's why they ask questions. If you don't want to answer, don't. Just say, "I don't want to answer that. It's too personal." On the other hand, there's no reason to hide the fact that you're adopted. So tell your parents what's going on. They can help you find the words to express your feelings about adoption in a way that makes you comfortable. The big surprise may be just how good this makes you feel.

Bad Influence

Dear *Help!*,

My friend and I have been best friends for three years. My mom and dad love her. The problem is that they also think she does improper things, which I will admit sometimes is true. They say she's a bad influence and want me to stop being friends with her.

Wanna Stay Friends

Your parents are afraid you'll start talking, acting, and thinking like your friend. So don't do it. Hold on to your own good judgment and don't *let* her influence you. And when your parents don't like the way your friend acts, tell her so. Say, "My parents don't allow swearing" or "My dad thought you were rude yesterday." Speak up yourself for what you believe is right. Be a good influence. If your friend can change her ways, maybe your parents will change their minds.

3

Best Friends

Dear *Help!*,

A long time ago I was best friends with my next-door neighbor, Katie. Now I have a new best friend. I still want to be friends with Katie, but not best friends. How can I tell her without hurting her?

Helpless in North Carolina

Well, the truth is, you've already hurt Katie. Her feelings were hurt as soon as you began spending more time with your new friend than you did with her. If you make an announcement like "You're not my best friend anymore," she's going to feel worthless. So give Katie the same kindness and attention you give the other girls you count as friends. If she asks why you are spending so much time with this new girl, say, "I like her a lot, but that doesn't mean you and I can't still be friends." Which is true.

We can still be friends.

Dear *Help!*,

I have a friend named Laura. She is good in art and is teacher's pet in almost everything. She is very nice and has many friends. When she plays with one of her other friends and not me, I get jealous and mad. I like Laura so much, and I want to be her best friend. But how can I when she has so many other friends?

Jealous

When you're crazy about a friend, it's natural to want that friend to be crazy about you. But you can't tell a friend how to feel. Laura *wants* to play with other girls. Getting jealous and angry won't change that. It will only make Laura think you're trying to hog her. So whenever you're with Laura, relax and enjoy yourself all you can. Chances are, she'll enjoy herself, too. Will that make you her best friend? Not necessarily. But it will make Laura happy to see your face when she sees it next.

Blabbermouth

Dear *Help!*,

I'm bad at keeping secrets. Every time someone tells me a secret, I blurt it out. I'm afraid my friends won't like me if I keep telling their secrets.

Elly

You're right. Your friends *won't* like you if you blab. So how do you stop?

Plan 1: The next time you're tempted to open your mouth to tell a friend's secret, imagine her face when she hears what you've done. If that doesn't help, go to . . .

Plan 2: When a friend says, "I'll tell you something if you promise to keep it a secret," plug your ears. Say, "Don't tell me, please! I can't keep my mouth shut. I'd rather keep your friendship than try to keep your secret."

Blushing

Dear *Help!*,

Whenever I get embarrassed my face gets real hot. When it happens in school, someone always says, "Hey! Your face is *so* red!" That makes me even redder.

Embarrassed

When you're embarrassed, your nerves send extra blood into the tiny blood vessels in your skin. Doctors call this *vasodilation* (VA-zo-di-LA-shun). The rest of us call it a blush. Blushing is a reflex—you do it without thinking—and that's why it's so hard to control. Keep in mind that all kids let their emotions show. Some do it by tears, some by temper. You blush. It's *natural*. As you get older, you won't be embarrassed as easily and will probably blush less. For now, when you feel a blush spreading, think of something cold, like ice water. That might help. And if a kid hoots, "Hey! Your face is *so* red!" just shrug and say, "I can't help it. I'm one of those kids who vasodilate a lot."

Bossy

Dear *Help!*,

Whenever I'm in school or somewhere else where we have to work in groups, everybody says that I'm bossy. I think it's because when I have an idea that I think would help, I want them to be quiet so I can tell them. That really doesn't help, so what do I do?

R.S.

For starters, don't talk too much. After you express an idea, wait till at least three other people have had their say before you open your mouth again. Do this even if you don't agree with what they say. Second, when the others are talking, listen. *Really* listen. Don't sit there rehearsing what you're going to say next. Finally, when you speak up again, be sure that what you say shows you've heard what the others said. Remember that sometimes the biggest difference between a bully and a leader is being able to l-i-s-t-e-n.

Boys

Dear *Help!*,

A boy in my class is my friend. We aren't boyfriend and girlfriend. We are just friends. Sometimes people make fun of us. It's really bugging me.

Erica

It's perfectly fine for girls and boys to be pals. Kids who don't understand that miss out on some wonderful friendships. Luckily, you're too smart to let that happen to you. Tell yourself this teasing is plain old peer pressure. Your best bet is to take the least popular but most effective advice of all—ignore it.

Boys

Dear *Help!*,

My friend and I like the same boy. I don't want to mess up our friendship, but I want the boy to like me, too. Is there any way I can get to know him without hurting my friend?

Baffled in Buffalo

There's no getting around the fact that you and your friend want the same thing, but it makes no sense to argue about who "gets" this boy. It's up to *him* to decide if he likes one of *you*. So tell your friend what you've said here: "I like Bob, too, but I don't want to mess up our friendship." Suggest to her that you get to know him together, and make a pact to put friendship first. If you want to talk to Bob during recess, invite your friend to come along. If you want to sit with Bob at lunch, save a spot for her as well. Most of all, don't do anything to hurt this boy's opinion of your friend. If you're kind and honest, you may find three can have a lot of fun.

Dear *Help!*,

Do you have any advice for when you like a boy and find yourself acting very weird around him?

Lost

Saying "relax and be yourself" is sort of like telling you to jump over the moon. It's the right answer, but 99 percent of girls find it impossible to do. So if you can't relax, do the next best thing. Don't try to impress him. Don't talk big—or smart or tough or sweety-sweet. It's better to seem a little goofy than to seem like a phony.

Bras

I'm going into fifth grade. All my friends wear bras. I asked my mom for one, but she said I didn't need one. I feel left out. Please don't tell me it doesn't matter. It does to me.

Left out

Start by telling your mom how you feel, and ask if you can spend your own money to buy a bra. If the answer's no, you might try layering your shirts and other tops. That way, no one can tell whether you're wearing a bra or not. You may still feel left out, and that's no fun, but you may also feel less self-conscious, and that could help.

Brothers & Sisters

Dear *Help!,*

I have a little brother who's six. I love him, but I'm constantly hearing "Don't fight with your brother" or "Be nice to your brother." I love my parents, but I have a terrible feeling in the pit of my stomach that they love him more.

Sick to My Stomach

Many, many big sisters have days when they feel as you do, but, truly, your parents don't love your brother more. Look at the families around you. Don't you see pretty much the same thing?

Most parents expect older kids to be understanding of their little brothers and sisters—to compromise, to share, to let them have their way. This has everything to do with how old you are and nothing at all to do with how much they love you. If it still doesn't feel that way, pick a quiet moment and ask your mom or dad for a hug. With their arms around you, your heart will know the truth.

Brothers & Sisters

Dear *Help!*,

My sister and I fight a lot. I'm not quite sure why, but when we don't fight I like to play with her, and I realize how much I love her. I want to stop fighting with her, but how?

Wanting to Stop

Sometimes fighting becomes a kind of habit. You do it without thinking, especially when you're bored. To stop the fights, make yourself aware of what you're doing. Tie a string on your finger or put a sticker on your hand. When bickering begins, the string will remind you that you don't want to fight. Grab on to your temper, and go find something fun and interesting to do instead. Finally, make a resolution to surprise your sister by doing one nice thing for her every week—something that will make her sit up, blink, and exclaim, "Gee, thanks!"

Dear *Help!,*

My sister is turning into a total teenager. I feel like we're growing apart. Please help me. She has started to talk on the phone endlessly and get interested in boys. Please don't tell me that this is all about growing up. I just need something to say to her.

Lonesome

Picking the right time to talk to her may be more important than some secret formula for what to say. Don't try to pull her away from her friends. Instead, look for quiet moments of the day when you're alone with your sister—say, when you're getting ready for bed or setting the table. Ask about her friends. Ask about the boys. Ask about anything you know she likes to talk about. Then listen. You may not care a whit about that stuff yourself, but it's a way to show you care about her. Truth is, this *is* all about growing up—but that's good news, not bad. It's good because it means your sister won't be like this forever. She'll continue to change, and so will you.

Brothers & Sisters

Dear *Help!*,

I have three younger sisters, and they are *triplets!* They are all two years old, and believe me they are not angels. I've got babysitting overload. I've tried talking to my parents and having a friend come and help me. What am I going to do about this impossible problem? I have no social life.

Kelly

It sounds as if your parents are as overloaded as you are—and in no mood to let you relax with a friend in your room while your sisters run them ragged on the other side of the door. Try this: Ask if you can sign up for some organized activities once or twice a week. If your parents think you're doing something worthwhile, they may be more willing to let you go. You might also ask if you can divide your time differently. If you babysit every Tuesday and Thursday afternoon, maybe you can have Wednesdays and Fridays off to go to a friend's.

Camp

Dear *Help!*,

This summer, my mom is going to make me go to a summer camp. I would much rather just stay at home and play with my friends and go to the beach with my family. I don't see why she wants to waste her money. But she says, "You'll have lots of fun." What can I do?

Reluctant Camper

A lot of parents don't want their kids "hanging around" all summer with little to do. Is that your mom's worry? If so, you could propose a schedule of activities that would keep you active and learning if you stayed at home. If she still wants you to go, decide you'll make the best of it. See if you can find a friend to go with you. Read about the camp. Choose your favorite activities. Then pack up your clothes and your sense of adventure, and have a smile ready for the girls you'll meet on the bus. By the end of the summer, they'll be your good friends.

Class Clown

Dear *Help!*,

I have great friends, but I always feel I have to prove myself to them by being funny. At the end of the year, I got an award for being most likely to become a comedian. I don't want to be remembered as class clown.

Too goofy

There's not a thing wrong with being funny or having a reputation as a comedian. All the same, you're smart to know you shouldn't hide behind the laughs. Great friends, like yours, love you for who you are—not because you entertain them. So start thinking of yourself as class scientist or class writer or whatever else you'd rather be. When you set off for school tomorrow, put a rubber ball in your pocket. When you feel yourself getting goofy, give it a squeeze. Pretend the ball is a clown's nose and tell yourself, "I'm not wearing this today."

Clothes

I love to dress up in fancy, wild, and casual clothes. I love putting together outfits. But whenever I put an outfit together, this girl in my class criticizes it, and I feel totally stupid. This girl acts like she's the queen of romance and fashion, even though we're only in the fourth grade.

Fashion Conscious

No way should you let this girl bully you into dressing her way! If you want to wear striped leggings with your polka-dot dress, do it; if you want to wear earrings made of Froot Loops, do that. Decide for yourself what you like. This doesn't mean you'll always come home happy with the outfit you wore. It does mean that learning to dress is about finding your *own* style—not learning to conform. You can tell that to the Queen of Fashion, too.

Competing

Dear *Help!,*

I'm on a soccer team. When we lost a couple of games, a few of the girls started saying, "Oh, we're going to lose the rest of the games," and I don't think that's true. How can I get them to think positive?

Wanting to Win

(1) Talk to the coach.

She may not realize how bad these other girls feel. So tell her. She may have all sorts of ideas that would help.

(2) Compliment your teammates.

Losing can be frustrating, and too often players criticize each other as a result. Do the reverse. Everyone has different strengths. A few words from you about a good play or a special talent could give a girl the confidence she lacks.

(3) Be a good example.

Keep your mind on the game. Don't think about the score or your mistakes or what your mom's doing on the sidelines. Play as hard in the last few minutes when you're five points behind as you did at the half when the game was tied. And play to win. You'll make good things happen for your team—and you could be the spark that makes other girls catch fire and play hard, too.

(4) Look for the small victories. When your friends are moaning about a loss, remind them of something good or funny that happened during the game—say, the moment little Mimi stole the ball from the big forward with the green shoes. It will help break the gloom and remind these girls that any game is a lot more than the final score.

Copycat

Dear *Help!*,

I have a friend who copies everything I do—my hair, my clothes, etc. It bothers me a lot. I painted my room light purple. A few months later, she wants her room painted again. She painted it the same EXACT shade of purple. Everyone should have her own style. Why copy me?

Mad in Massachusetts

Because she has no confidence in her own taste—and a lot of confidence in yours. She admires you! What you need to do is tell her nicely that you don't like being copied, but you'd be glad to give her advice when she's getting her hair cut or picking out clothes or anything else. Then—and this is important—when she makes a choice, compliment her. Let her know you respect her choices. Then maybe she can begin to respect them herself.

Crybaby

Dear *Help!*,

I'm too sensitive. I cry over everything. Then people make fun of me. I try not to cry, but I can't help it!

Crybaby

It sounds as if you've got more feelings inside than you can hold. See what happens if you put some of them into a journal. Write every day. Write about things that have happened to you. Write about people you know. As you express yourself on paper, you'll be untangling thoughts and thinking to yourself about problems you face. This may help you express your feelings to other people in words. The more you can say in words, the less you may need to say in tears.

Disabled

Dear *Help!*,

I am handicapped and just moved to a new school. Suddenly, I am getting special treatment from other kids. I HATE THAT. I wish they'd stop treating me like I'm broken.

Elsie

These kids may be going about it the wrong way, but the fact is, they're trying to be nice. So talk to your teacher. She can introduce the subject of disabilities in class. Once your classmates get the basic facts, they'll be more able to treat you naturally. You should also practice speaking up for yourself. There isn't a thing wrong with telling a kid in a friendly way, "Thanks very much, but I can do this myself."

Divorce

Dear *Help!*,

My parents fight a lot. It always makes me scared that they're going to get a divorce. Mom will say, "No, honey, we're fine." But then I listen through the door to the basement or the laundry chute. What should I do?

Upset

When parents fight, it can be *so* hard and *so* scary. Yet some arguments can help solve a problem. Others go away when a situation changes. Your mom might be right—the marriage could be fine. For now, you might feel better if you stopped eavesdropping on these fights. Make yourself listen to the radio instead. If you can't help but overhear your parents' angry words, let them know how this made you feel. It's O.K. to ask for reassurance. It's O.K. to ask if they're going to a counselor to resolve their differences, too. Just remember that if there's a problem with the marriage, only your mom and dad can fix it. No one can do it for them—not even you.

Divorce

Dear *Help!*,

My parents are divorced. My dad lives in New Mexico. He is always promising that he will call me, write me, or come and visit, but he never does, and that hurts me.

Hurt

Write him a letter and say so, as plainly as you can. Does your dad realize how many promises he's broken? List them. Does he think his visits and phone calls don't matter to you? Tell him they matter a lot. Why does he keep talking about tomorrow? Say you need to know he loves you today. It might do you good just to write this sort of letter, and it might well do your father good to receive it.

Dear *Help!*,

My parents are getting a divorce. I only see my dad on Saturday, and I do not think this is fair. It's hard to do this with my dad. My sisters and I are sad when he leaves for a week. How can I deal with this change?

A Girl Who Misses Her Dad

This *is* hard—terribly. Talk to both your parents about how you feel and say you'd like to have more time with your dad. Can you and your sisters spend one night a week at your dad's, or at least have dinner with him? Or can you stay with him on Sundays every other week? These are questions you have a perfect right to ask. On days you can't see your dad, call him and fill him in on what happened that day—and do the same with your mom when you're staying at your dad's.

Divorce

My mother and father got divorced about five years ago. I live with my mom. I would like to get married and have kids some day, but I'm afraid that I might get divorced and I wouldn't want my kids to go through what I had to. I know it's a long way off, but I think about it.

Worried

P.S. I talked to my mother about it, but she didn't know what to say.

A girl can inherit a lot of things from her parents—the color of her skin, the shape of her nose. But a divorce? No. No way. There's just no reason that your future has to be like your parents' past. Make up your mind to take what you've learned from your parents' mistakes and use it to avoid mistakes of your own. For now, pack up the question "Should I get married?" and store it in a corner of your brain. When the time comes to take it out, you'll know the answer.

Fame

Dear *Help!*,

I am ten years old. I live in Tennessee. I know what I want to be: an actress and a supermodel. I am really determined to be those things, but when you live in an unfamous state like Tennessee it's hard to be recognized for your talent and become a big star.

Beth

Your average Famous Person started out life as a regular kid—a kid who was good at some things and not so good at others, living an unfamous life in an unfamous place. A kid, in other words, exactly like you. So don't worry a bit about being from Tennessee. What will matter to you are things like brains, talent, determination, looks, luck, and plain hard work. Just stick this thought in your pocket: Happiness doesn't come from seeing your face on the newsstands. Happiness comes from loving what you do and liking who you are.

29

Fear

Dear *Help!*,

I'm afraid of getting kidnapped. Sometimes I go too far, like when people are nice to me in the village shops, I think they're trying to kidnap me. I have bad dreams about being kidnapped at least twice a week. I talk to people about it, and that helps a little.

Scared in Kansas

(1) Keep talking.

It *does* help, you're right. Scary thoughts and dreams lose power when you think about them out loud with someone you trust. An adult can also remind you that, despite awful stories you may see in the news, abductions by strangers are very, VERY rare.

(2) Don't bite off more than you can chew. If going to the village alone scares you, don't do it. Instead, ask your parents to help you master your fear bit by bit. Go to town with them. Let them introduce you to clerks they know. Locate the public phones. Talk about what you should do if you ever feel threatened. Where should you go? To whom should you turn? Get to know all the public places you might visit. When you feel ready, practice going into the stores alone while your mom or dad is nearby. After that, do some errands with a friend.

Chip away at the fear little by little, and give your confidence a chance to grow. (3) Remember, you're NOT powerless. Follow the three W's: Never go anyplace with anyone unless your mom or dad knows WHERE you are, WHOM you're with, and WHEN you'll be back. Keep in mind that if you find yourself in a situation that makes you nervous, you have every right to tell an adult how you feel and ask for help. Finally, tell yourself that you have a lot of control over your own safety. Because you do.

Freckles

Dear *Help!*,

I don't think I'm pretty. I have a ton of freckles all over my face.

Not Pretty in New York

When you look in the mirror, all you see are your freckles. Yet chances are, your friends hardly see them at all. They look at you and see—well, *you*. They see the brightness in your eyes, the curve of your smile, the expression on your face— your whole personality shining through your features. That's where beauty lies, not in how close you come to looking like a model. Try to believe that. And this, too: Almost everyone likes freckles except the girls who have them.

Friendless

Dear *Help!*,

I have no friends at school. Sometimes girls will be my friend, then use me and leave me. Everyone around me has friends. I feel so lonely sometimes I cry. I'm really a nice person but no one likes me. I can't figure out why. I feel so worthless.

All Alone

Look around you one more time. Do you see anyone else who's alone a lot? How about the quiet girl from the next class who stands by herself on the playground? Try offering some friendly words to her.

Sign up for some after-school activities, too. A girl who ignores you now might see you differently if she learns you're as interested in tree frogs as she is. Finally, look for friends outside of school. Take a class in ballet, karate, art, or whatever else sounds fun. The more active you are, the happier you'll be—and the better chance you'll have of meeting a girl who's smart enough to see what a terrific friend you'd make.

Frustrating Friends

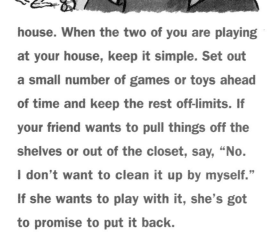

Dear *Help!*,

I have a friend who doesn't like to clean up. Whenever we play with things, she goes home and leaves the cleaning to me. When I tell her we have to clean up, she says, "Let's leave it out and play with it tomorrow." Or she stuffs it in the closet, like, "I'll hold it while you shut the door." I've tried confronting her, but she says, "That's the way I am."

The Maid

If you and your friend plan to play a game that involves a lot of stuff, go to her house. When the two of you are playing at your house, keep it simple. Set out a small number of games or toys ahead of time and keep the rest off-limits. If your friend wants to pull things off the shelves or out of the closet, say, "No. I don't want to clean it up by myself." If she wants to play with it, she's got to promise to put it back.

Dear *Help!*,

Whenever my friend comes over to my house, she always has to get what she wants or she goes home. I try to do the same thing at her house, but all she says is "Fine. Go home."

Jennifer

Your friend is bullying you, and if you really want her to stop, you'll have to call her bluff the way she calls yours. The next time she threatens to walk out, keep your cool and say nicely, "Maybe it *would* be best if you left. Maybe we shouldn't play together today." Then go to the closet and hand this gal her coat. The message will be very clear. You aren't going to let her win an argument with threats.

Gangs

Dear *Help!*,

I'm in fourth grade. I have to go to a certain junior high school when I'm in seventh. My sister and I are scared to go there. My sister has to go there next year and, boy, is she scared. Why? Because there are gangs! We've heard of these gangs! We're so scared!

Scared Stiff

Rumors can be scarier than facts. So for starters, work with your parents and sister to find out what's really going on in this school. Talk to the principal, the teachers, the police, other parents. Talk to kids who go there. Are gangs really a menace? If so, what's the community doing to solve this terrible problem, and how can you and your family help? Also, what advice do these people have for kids like you? Should you stay away from certain places or avoid wearing certain clothes? The more you know, the safer you'll be, whatever the situation. Most of all, be sure to choose the right friends—friends who want to keep as far away from gangs as you do.

Gossip

Dear *Help!*,

Some of my friends are talking behind my back. Whenever I'm around them, they act as sweet and innocent as a cupcake. It bothers me to think they would do that.

Truly Bothered

You're right to be bothered. If your friends have a bone to pick with you, they should come to you and say so. *Psst-psst*-ing about it with other kids is simply two-faced. Your best bet is to talk to these girls honestly. Try not to accuse them. Instead, *tell* and *ask*. Tell them what you heard. Tell them how it made you feel. Ask them straight out, "Did you really say those things about me?" Perhaps you can talk it out and clear the air. And if you can't? If your friends still aren't honest with you? Then you can't trust them—and it's time to start looking for friends you can.

Grades

Dear *Help!*,

My mom expects A's and some B's in my school grades. But on my last report card my math grade went from an A+ to a B–. I told her things were just getting harder. But she won't let go. My math teacher said, "Don't push her," but Mom won't listen. I feel she expects too much.

frustrated in Colorado

You, your mom, and your teacher should have a conference. Discuss how and what you should study each day, and the amount of time it should take. If the three of you can come up with a study plan that addresses your mother's concerns, maybe she will agree not to push you about your grades. Then it's up to you to follow the plan. If you truly try your best, you can be proud of yourself no matter what grade you get—and your mom should be proud of you, too.

Gross

On my bus, there's this really gross kid who says things that are so sick it's embarrassing to tell anyone, even my mother. I'll go to the front of the bus, but he'll follow me. Then he'll say he's sorry, but two seconds later he'll do it again.

amie

DING!DING!DING!DING! The alarm's going off—and it's *loud.* Please, please tell your parents about this kid. Ask them to come with you to talk to the principal. What's happening here doesn't sound like a goofy gross-out ("The worms crawl in, the worms crawl out . . ." and stuff like that). It sounds more like an assault. The school should know about it, his parents should know, the bus driver should know. This boy's got to hear it loud and clear from all sides: Either he leaves you alone or he walks.

39

Haircut

Dear *Help!*,

I have a short haircut. A lot of kids at my school ask me the same question: "Are you a boy or a girl?" In front of all my friends! It really embarrasses me, but I hate long hair and I hate dresses.

a girl

Don't think for a minute that these kids have really mistaken you for a boy. They're teasing you, plain and simple. The best answer to "Are you a boy or a girl?" is "If you don't know the difference, you better talk to your mom."

Home-schooled

Dear *Help!*,

I'm in fifth grade, and I just started home-schooling. Everywhere I go, people have conversations about school. I feel embarrassed because they don't understand about home-schooling. They say, "That's weird" or "Don't you miss your friends?" What should I say?

Elisabeth

People will take their cue from you. If you look at your shoes and mumble, "My mom makes me do it," they'll think you've got something to be embarrassed about.

Look them in the eye instead. Explain how home-schooling works. Explain what you like about it and what you don't. For example: "I like getting my studying done more quickly and having more free time. I do miss my friends, but I still get to see them in the afternoons." There are hundreds of thousands of kids home-schooled in America today—so, you see, it's really *not* weird at all.

Homework

Dear *Help!*,

I'm not very organized. Sometimes I don't do my homework, and I'm in deep water with the alligators. Please help me find a way to be more organized and help me to remember to do my homework!

Unorganized

Here's a recipe for getting your work done using some very basic ingredients:

1 spiral notebook

1 calendar

1 alarm clock

a dash of self-reliance

Step 1. The notebook:

Label a spiral notebook "Homework." Take it to school every day. When you get an assignment, record it here. Draw an alligator on the cover to remind you what will happen if you forget.

Step 2. The desk:

Take a look at your desk or work area. Do you see loose papers? Scrunchies? A peach pit? Off they go. There should be nothing on it but a calendar and your schoolbooks. Period.

Step 3. The time:

Set a certain time for doing your home-work, and do it at that time every day. If you find yourself cheating, set an alarm clock when you come in from school. When it goes off, you go to your desk and sit down. (It doesn't hurt to ask Mom or Dad to encourage and remind you, too.)

Step 4. The planning:

So you're at your desk. Before you do anything else, read over your assignments and write the deadlines on your calendar. Which ones are due tomorrow? Which ones are due after that? If you have a big project, break it into smaller pieces: "Go to the library." "Read about snails." "Write report." "Do graphs." Write each step on a day of your calendar, too.

Step 5. The doing:

First do the assignments that are due tomorrow. Then check your calendar and decide what you should do next. You're the boss. Now follow your own orders.

"I Hate My Name"

Dear *Help!*,

My name is Rosemary. I hate my name. All my friends have cool names. All the people I read about have good names, too. I feel like I'm the only one in the world without a good name. I want to change it, but my parents won't let me.

Rosemary

Is there a nickname you like? Rose or Rosie or Ro? If so, ask your friends and teacher to call you that. Remember, too, that names go in and out of fashion every bit as much as clothes. In 1900, the name Mildred was hot. In 1925, Betty was in the top ten. In 1970, Michelle seemed to be everywhere. Ashley came along in the 1980s. The point is this: "Rosemary" may seem geeky to you today, but it could be the coolest name on the planet tomorrow. So tell yourself you're a trendsetter. You have your own style, your own brain—your own name.

Klutz

I'm a klutz. Every time I turn around I break something, whether it's a bone in my body or my mom's best vase. What can I do?

Queen of clumsiness

It's a good bet that you aren't clumsy because you're a klutz. You're clumsy because you're growing. When a girl's in a growth spurt, her hands and feet get bigger before her arms and legs do. Till her arms and legs catch up, she has less control of those big hands and feet. So what should you do? Keep active in sports.

Slow down by the china cabinet. Be patient. You're going to grow out of this.

45

Left Out

Dear *Help!*,

I have two good friends. One, in front of my face, will say to the other, "Do you want to spend the night?" The other will say, "O.K." I don't have the courage to say that I feel sad and left out. Please give me some advice.

Feeling left out

Ugh! This is so rude! Your friends should have better sense than to do this—better sense and kinder hearts. If you can't find the courage to express your feelings directly, try this: The next time you ask one of these girls to do something special, do it by phone. Say, "I didn't ask you at school because I didn't want to hurt Mary's feelings. I really hate it when someone does that to me." If she doesn't take the hint, she doesn't care about your feelings. Start looking around for friends who will.

Lies

Dear *Help!,*

One of my best friends is always making up stories about things at school, and what she can and can't do. She is a very nice person, and I like playing with her, but I never know when she is telling the truth.

fed up

It sounds as if your friend doesn't think much of herself and thinks she has to lie to be liked. She's making a big mistake. Her lies will cost her friends, not make them. So tell her how you feel. Say, "You're a great person, but when you say you can speak German, and I know you can't, it really bothers me. It makes me wonder about everything you say. I don't care if you speak German, but I do care if you're dishonest." She may get angry. She may also think twice before she tells a lie again.

Locker Room

Dear *Help!*,

This year, I'm in seventh grade, and we have to change into gym clothes every day for Phys Ed. I'm not very thin, and we change in the locker room in front of other girls. I really don't feel comfortable about doing this! That may sound dumb because we're all girls, but that's how I feel.

Uncomfortably Shy

It doesn't sound dumb at all! Changing in a locker room is very different from changing at home. The best thing is to get it over with as quickly as you can.

Don't slow yourself down looking for girls who might be looking at you. Pay attention to what *you're* doing instead. Tell yourself that half the girls are worried about getting to their next class on time, and the other half feel just like you.

Mooch

Dear *Help!*,

When my best friend and I go to a candy store, she asks me to buy her something. I do. But she never pays me back.

always buying

A lot of girls find it hard to say no, but that's precisely the word you need here. This girl is taking advantage of you. The next time she says, "I would gladly pay you Tuesday for a Tootsie Roll today," say, "No. I'm not going to lend you any money until you pay me the $2.60 you owe me." She may give you some grief; don't give her a cent. Maybe the next time you go shopping, she'll remember to bring her purse.

Movies

Dear *Help!*,

My mom is very strict about what movies I see. All the movies that she lets me see are too babyish for me. I'm ten, and she barely lets me see some movies rated PG!

W.D.

Your mom has her own ideas about what's right for a girl your age. There's nothing you can do to change that— which is why you're feeling so frustrated. What you *can* do is change your mom's opinion of how mature you are, in the way you fulfill responsibilities and handle disagreements just like this one. Will acting mature this afternoon get your mom to let you go to the movie tonight? No. But it could make her stop and think, "Wow, my daughter's really growing up."

Munching

Dear *Help!*,

I'm ten, and I'm a little overweight. I tend to watch TV a little more than I should, and the TV room is right next to the kitchen. When I watch TV I tend to eat things like chocolate chips and potato chips. I mean, I have an after-school snack, but it seems when I munch I never get full.

A Little Chubby

You're a smart girl to realize that your munching is part of your TV habit. Now, here's what to do. When you come in from school, get yourself a snack—one good snack that fills you up. Then tell yourself, "No more food till dinner." If you watch TV, give yourself something to do with your hands besides eat. Play solitaire or write in your diary or tickle the cat. Better yet, don't watch TV at all. Ride your bike or kick a soccer ball or walk the dog. Instead of gaining weight, you'll be taking it off—and you may have a lot more fun to boot.

New Glasses

Dear *Help!*,

I just got reading glasses, and I hate them! Everyone in my class thinks they're cute. How can I grow to like them?

Frustrated

Glasses feel odd when you first wear them. Everything seems brighter. Even the pencil on your desk suddenly seems to stand out. And, of course, when you look at yourself in a mirror, the glasses seem to stand out, too. You may feel like a Martian—and think you look like one, too. Truly, this is often a matter of giving your eyes time to adjust. Your friends say your glasses are cute. For now, why not believe them?

Old Car

Dear *Help!*,

This may sound funny, but, well, you see, my family has had an old Cadillac for ten years and I love it very much. But my dad said since it doesn't run anymore, he's going to take it to a place where they are going to smash it up, so we can get some money for it. I don't want my dad to do that!

a sad friend of a car

Good times rub off on the objects people touch and care for every day. A car becomes more than a car. It's the family trip you took last summer. It's the day your sister spilled Coke on her head in the backseat. Still, what's the better future for the car you've loved so well? **(a)** It sits in your driveway, rusting until parts fall off. Or **(b)** it gets recycled, and its steel may be used again in a new car, which another little girl can spill Coke in. Really, the answer's pretty clear. So take a picture of your old car, then say good-bye. Let the tow truck have the metal. You have the memories.

Only Child

Dear *Help!*,

I'm an only child. As fun as everyone thinks it is, sometimes it's lonely. I've asked my mom and dad if they would ever have another baby, but they never answer.

Lonely

If you've told your parents how much you'd like a brother or sister, you've done about all a girl can do to get one. Now the decision is up to them. Don't sit around waiting. Check out the rest of your family—your larger family. Do you have cousins near your own age? Get to know them better. If your cousins live far away, ask your parents if you can invite them for a visit in the summer. How about second cousins? Aunts and uncles? Make a friend of everyone in the family you especially like. You'll feel less like the only kid in a family of three and more like one of the clan.

Partners

Dear *Help!*,

In school we have partners. My partner makes me do all the work, and she just copies what I write.

Doing All the Work

If this girl is just lazy, tell her straight out how you feel. If she's copying because she's struggling with the material, take a deep breath, try to be patient, and give her some help. In either case, talk to your teacher. Partnerships are rarely equal, and she knows that. But she should have ideas for how to make this one more fair.

Peer Pressure

Dear *Help!*,

Most of my friends hang out in one big group. Somehow they end up talking about someone—she's ugly or she's nasty, etc. I don't like this. If I try to talk to my friends about it, they get real angry at me!

Mixed up

People do all sorts of things when they're in a group that they wouldn't do alone. It's as if they think there's one way to be—to look, to talk, to think. If a girl's different—*boom!* The group is saying mean things and sometimes doing mean things, too. You're right not to like it, and doubly right to speak up. If you can find the courage to hold your own opinions, maybe the other girls will wake up to what they're doing and feel ashamed. As they should.

Pentecostal

Dear *Help!*,

I belong to a Pentecostal church. I can't wear pants, cut my hair, or wear jewelry or makeup. A lot of people tease me. They call me Ms. Conservative and Long-Haired Smart Aleck—and I'm not a smart aleck.

Picked on

Too many kids spend too much time on the Science of Cool—how to dress cool, act cool, be cool. It makes them blind. They can't see a nice human being standing three feet away if she's wearing the "wrong" look. What do you do with kids like this? You can try explaining nicely that the way you dress is part of your religion. It's possible that some kids don't understand this, and would stop teasing you if they did. You can also go with your parents to talk to your teacher, who may have her own ways of getting these kids to lay off. In any case, stick with the kids who care about what you're like *inside* and respect you for standing up for your beliefs.

57

Pets

Dear *Help!*,

I love my dog. I can't remember a time when he hasn't been there. He's twelve. So am I. He has a hard time breathing, and his hearing is nearly gone. His eyesight is bad, too. My mom and brother are thinking of having him put to sleep. They say he is in a lot of pain. I would have no problem putting him to sleep if he could tell me that's what he wants. I can't stand the thought of losing him! Please help!

Hopeful

No one can tell you whether you should put your dog to sleep. Hard as it is, you have to make up your own mind about that. But talk to your vet. Does she think your dog's in pain? If so, is there anything that can be done to help? How long does your vet think your dog will live? Ask all the questions you can. Use the answers and the love you feel for your dog to help you make a choice.

Dear *Help!*,

I have a hamster named Yo. When I bought him, he was nice, but now he's really mean. I brought him to school for a class, and he bit two people, including my teacher. Now everyone calls him Lucifer!

Stumped

Put yourself in Yo's shoes. Or cage, rather. A trip to school can be a scary thing for a pet. Imagine being in a strange classroom. The world is a wall of new faces. Loud voices boom. Big fingers waggle at you through the bars. An enormous hand appears and grabs for you . . . ***EEEEK!*** No girl should keep a pet that bites, but if Yo has calmed down since you brought him home, he probably just can't take crowds. So give him what he needs: a quiet room and a second chance.

Piano Lessons

Dear *Help!*,

I hate piano lessons! They are so hard! They make me so mad! I stay on the same page for such a long time. My younger sister is very good at it and progresses quickly.

Unhappy

If you sit down to play hating the piano, your anger will build with each wrong note till you can't see the music in front of your face. So wipe your sister out of your mind. Tell yourself it's O.K. to go at your own rate. Then ask your teacher if you can learn a piece that you especially like. Practice this and only this till you can play it easily and well. Play it loud. Play it soft. Use the pedals. Sing along. Have fun with it. Then go back to your regular book. The next time your head's about to pop off with frustration, play a couple bars of your special piece. The music will soothe your temper, restore your confidence, and remind you that there's joy to be had if you stick with it.

Picky Parent

Let me get straight to the point. My mom is too picky. I'll get my room sparkling clean and dust our furniture almost perfect, but she seems to always find something wrong. Sometimes I spend my whole weekend doing chores. Help!

Tired

When you have a chore to do, talk to your mom *before* you start about how she wants it done. Can you dust around the clock, or should you lift it up and dust beneath it? Can you sweep the floor or do you need to vacuum, too? Once you know what your mom wants, do it, and do it carefully. Don't rush it. The job may take more time than you wish it did, but when you finish you'll be finished. You won't have to do it twice.

61

Pink

Dear *Help!*,

My room is almost all pink. I don't care for pink anymore. When we moved in I was six, and I loved pink. I got pink curtains, carpet, desk, and bed. I want to get new colors, but my parents say no. When I walk in I feel so weird. It's just too little for me now.

Sick of pink

Adding other colors to your room will cut the pink and give the room a jazzier, older feel. Try dark colors, like dark purples and blues, even black. Scrounge around the house. Put a blanket or an old table-cloth at the foot of your bed. Spend your own money to get some small pillows for the bed and a throw rug for the carpet. Cover the desktop with a blotter or a big sheet of paper. Sew or pin buttons onto the curtains like polka dots. Finally, ask yourself if there are other things in the room that make it look too young. If so, store them away.

Popularity

Dear *Help!*,

When I'm at school, very unpopular people come and ask me to play with them. I don't want to because I'm afraid I'll get unpopular.

Confused in Fort Worth

Being unpopular isn't like the flu—you don't catch it from someone who's got it. Still, it's certainly possible that the snobs in your class will make fun of you if you play with someone they think you should ignore. So here's your choice: (a) You can ignore the kids the snobs ignore and be a snob, too. Or (b) you can play with the kids you want to play with. If you choose (a) you'll be safe from the snobs. If you choose (b) you'll be free of them, and on your way to leading your own life.

Race

Dear *Help!*,

I just moved to a new town. I am black. In my old town, there were plenty of black people, but here there are hardly any. People look at me weird. Some kids tease me. I even think that some parents don't want to let their kids play with me and my little sisters. How am I ever going to make friends?

different

Being the new girl on the block is never easy. If people are prejudiced against your race, it can be one of the loneliest and most painful things in the world. But there *are* things you can do:

(1) Take another look at your neighbors, and talk—*really* talk—to your mom and dad. Do they see as much prejudice in this town as you do? Do *they* think you can make friends here? If so, where do they think you should start? Can they help you break the ice? Let your mom and dad know how you feel, and ask for their help.

(2) You might also try to hook up with other black kids in your area. There must

be some place African-American kids get together—a church, say, or a community organization. It will feel good to talk to other girls who know what it's like to be black in a white town—to share experiences and to exchange advice and tips of all sorts. Having black friends might make you feel less alone in this new place, even if you don't see them every day.

(3) Get involved in organized activities, both in and outside of school. Get out on the soccer field. Get a seat in the orchestra. Join the science club. The girls you meet will share your interests, and when you're sitting side by side trying to hit C-sharp, race will matter a whole lot less.

(4) Put your favorite photo of yourself on your bureau. *That's who you are.* Whenever you get one of those "weird" looks, tell yourself that. Remember the heroes who've fought in this country's battle with racism, and let confidence shine in your eyes. Sooner or later friends will come along who see and admire that.

Race

Dear *Help!*,

I have some black friends and like them equally as my white. My dad hurts my feelings because he uses a terrible word when he talks about blacks. I don't want to grow up being prejudiced! I feel very uncomfortable. Please help!

NOT Prejudiced

The next time your dad uses a racist word, tell him you don't like it. Say, "Please don't use that word. It's racist." If he keeps it up, or gets mad, leave the room. You can't stop your dad from talk-ing this way if he's determined to do it, but you can let him know that he doesn't speak for you. You don't believe that people who are different from you are worth less than you. Say it firmly. Say it often. Let it guide your life.

Daddy, please don't use that word!

Roller Coaster

Dear *Help!*,

When my family goes on a roller coaster, I get nervous. I'm scared of high heights and going upside down. I don't know how to cure it!

one scared-stiff girl

There's nothing odd about being scared on a roller coaster. You're supposed to be scared. That's the whole point! Some people like that scary feeling. You don't. That's perfectly O.K. A girl who goes on carnival rides isn't braver or better than a girl who doesn't. If you dread getting on a ride, don't make yourself do it.

Second Choice

Dear *Help!*,

I know two girls. They're in my class and they're always together. I like them, but they treat me like the odd-ball, the second choice. When one's out, I'm the one the other turns to in class. But it makes me feel bad, to be the second choice.

Second Choice

Hanging around a pair like this can make a girl miserable. They're just too wrapped up in each other to care about how you feel. Yet it seems they're your first choice of friends—and that's what has to change.

Don't wait around for them to notice you. Make up your mind to get to know some other girls better. You'll feel a lot less left out if you're busy laughing and talking and working with someone else.

Sharing a Room

Dear *Help!*,

I have to share a room with my sister. She bothers me a lot. When I want to sleep at night, she keeps talking to me. If she's gone and I try to get some privacy, she comes barging in on me. I've tried talking to my mom, but the only other room that isn't occupied is the garage.

Going Nuts

You can't sleep in the Chevy, so better try a Sisters' Constitution instead. Ask your mom to sit down with you and your sister to write up a list of promises the two of you agree to make to each other about the room. For example: "I won't talk after lights-out." Or "I always have the right to enter my own room, but if the door's closed I'll knock first." Then both of you should sign the paper and hang it on your bedroom wall. This idea won't give you a room of your own, but it might well give you a better roommate.

Sleepovers

Dear *Help!*,

Whenever I go to a slumber party everyone disagrees. Some girls want to stay awake and some want to sleep. Then lots of people cry.

Sleepy and mad

The solution is to have one room for girls who want to sleep and another for girls who don't. Girls can lay out their sleeping bags in the snooze room when they first arrive. As the night goes on, sleepy girls can go to bed one by one, and party girls can party without stepping on someone's head.

Eight Tips for a Super Sleepover

1. Don't invite too many girls. The party will get wild, and your friends are more likely to break up into cliques. Five guests max.

2. Have at least three big activities planned for the night. Don't try to wing it by thinking up activities as you go. Trouble starts when guests get bored.

3. Check your supplies. If you plan to make cookies, buy the chocolate chips the day before.

4. Discuss the rules for the party with your parents before the party begins. Set a time for lights-out, and announce it to your friends soon after they arrive.

5. Be sure to have extra board games and a deck of cards sitting around the party room. They'll give you something to turn to if any of those big activities you planned don't work out.

6. No rough stuff. A pillow fight may sound like fun. In real life, girls get shaken up and things get broken.

7. Beware of truth-or-dare. A game that encourages girls to tell secrets leads to embarrassment and humiliation. Skip it.

8. And, of course, let sleeping girls sleep.

Smart

Dear *Help!*,

I'm smart, with a straight-A average, and friendly to almost everyone. Just one problem: Everyone thinks I'm a goody-goody. Some kids think it's not cool to be smart, but I know they have to be wrong. Right?

Emily

Right. In every school, there's a group of kids who spend their time cutting down achievers and trying to convince people that nothing's cooler than being bored. Hooey. The truth is, it's a ton of fun to use your brain at school. Good grades lead a million places you want to go. Boredom leads nowhere. So if you're not showing off—and it doesn't sound like you are—then you've got every reason to be proud. You're on the right road. Stick with it.

Smelly

Dear *Help!*,

One of my really good friends smells like a fish. I don't know how to tell her. What should I do?

Amy

Telling a friend she smells can be tricky. The problem comes up most often with girls who don't realize they have to bathe more frequently as they get older. In your friend's case, the smell may have something to do with what her family eats. It could have something to do with cultural traditions as well. If the smell is strong enough that you and other kids notice it and dislike it, she ought to know that. So who should tell her? Try talking to your teacher or the school nurse. They probably have more experience with situations like this, and can find a kind and private way to offer this girl a tip.

Sports

Dear *Help!*,

I'm twelve and I love sports. My town does not let girls play many sports. For instance, the boys play regular baseball, but the girls play softball, which uses a bigger and softer ball. The boys get uniforms, and all the girls get are T-shirts. I know many other girls feel the same way, but I don't know what to do.

Sports Lover

Write a letter to the head of the baseball program pointing out how girls are being treated differently from boys and suggesting—politely—that this isn't right. Ask all the other girls to sign your letter. Make lots of photocopies. Mail the original to the head of the program, and a photocopy to every other adult who has a say in it, including all the coaches. (Ask your parents to review the letter and help you gather names and addresses.) Your letter's sure to get people talking, and that's the first step toward change.

Dear *Help!*,

I'm no good at sports, and I hate them. But my best friend likes to play sports, and so do all the other kids in my class. At recess, I just sit out and watch. My teacher told me to just join in. I did, but I'm not good, so people yelled at me.

Bad at Sports

Do something else! Swing on the swings. Jump rope. Play jacks or hopscotch or four square. Play Chinese jump rope or cat's cradle. Read a book or write a poem. Chat with other kids who aren't in the game. Do anything but sit and watch. If you still feel left out, ask your friends and family to work with you on basic sports skills a little every day. Practice throwing and catching balls. Practice kicking and dribbling them. Play the games they play at school. After a month, rejoin the games at recess. You'll still make mistakes—everyone does, including the kids who yelled at you. But the ball will feel more natural in your hands, you'll do better, and you'll enjoy it more.

Stepfamilies

Dear *Help!*,

My parents are divorced and Mom's getting married again. Her boyfriend's acting like my real father, telling me what to do, and what I can and can't have. What should I do?

Lauren

It's hard to have someone act like a dad when you don't feel like a daughter. So talk to your mom. Tell her that you know you'll have to obey her boyfriend eventually, but ask if you can have some extra time to get to know him better before you do. Ask for their patience.

Then make it a point to do some fun things with your future stepdad. Go to a movie together. Throw a baseball in the yard. As he becomes more a part of your life, it will seem more natural for him to enforce the rules. And don't worry that you're betraying your father by getting to know your stepfather. Your dad is still your dad. Nothing is going to change that.

Dear *Help!*,

My father just remarried. I have two stepbrothers, one older and one younger than me. I try to think of them as brothers, but as much as I try to love them, it seems like we fight all the time.

Trying in California

It sounds as if you were an only child before your dad remarried. That means you're learning to be a sister and a stepsister at the same time. That's a big, big change! Plus, your brothers may be struggling with how they feel about the new family and taking it out on you. So confide in your dad, mom, and stepmom, and ask for advice on getting along with the boys. But be patient. If you don't love these guys yet, that's O.K. Love can't be delivered in a moving van like a new sofa. Love grows. *You're trying to love.* That's the absolute best thing in the world you can do.

Teased

Dear *Help!*,

I'm not very pretty and not at all popular. I don't have very many friends. Last year some kids teased me and even stole some of my stuff. The torment was every day, and I'm not exaggerating. My mom says they did it because they were jealous, but I have nothing that they could be jealous of. Please help.

Desperate for Respect in Oklahoma

The adults who run your school are responsible for making it a safe and decent place for every child, including you. When teasing gets this vicious, it's time for them to step in and call a halt. Ask your mom or dad to go with you to talk to your teacher and the principal. Is this tattling? No. It's more like calling the police. If these kids have stolen things from you and torment you daily, you deserve protection and they deserve to be exposed. You sound like a nice girl. This mean crew would be wise to envy you that.

Teddy Bear

Dear *Help!*,

I am in the seventh grade and I still sleep with a teddy bear. I really like sleeping with him. I feel kind of safe. My teddy bear is like a best friend to me. I've slept with him since I was three. It's a habit I wish I could stop. It prevents me from sleeping over at friends', and having them sleep over with me.

help needed

If you don't make a big deal about your bear, your friends won't, either. When you go somewhere to spend the night, stick your teddy bear in the bottom of your bag. When it's time to go to sleep, pull him out. If your friend says, "You still sleep with a *bear*?" say, "Sometimes. He's cute." Let it go at that. You can say the same thing when a friend sleeps over with you. Who knows? Your friend may sigh with relief, dig into her bag, and grab a fuzzy friend of her own.

Too Busy

Dear *Help!*,

When I get home from school, I have so many things to do! (1) I have to do my homework. (There is usually a *ton* of it.) (2) Practice the piano. (3) Practice the violin. (4) Study for a test (usually). I don't have time to do anything fun! I don't want to quit anything.

A Girl in Solon, Ohio

Make up an after-school schedule. Set aside a time to study, a time to practice, *and* a time to have fun. Be very official about this. Write down, **"5-6 p.m. Have FUN!"** And when the clock strikes five (or whatever time you pick), take a break from your studies and your music and goof off. A little free time will make you feel a lot less busy, and you'll go at your tasks—**1, 2, 3, 4**—with a fresh brain and good spirits.

Too Tall

Dear *Help!*,

Some people say I'm smart, funny, and nice. All people say I'm tall. Boys say, "So how's the weather up there? Ha ha."

too Tall for words

Girls start growing faster than boys at about age ten. By twelve, girls tend to be taller. A girl with tall parents may be a lot taller—and feel like a stork in a flock of ducks. But take heart. This is not going to last forever. By the time you're out of middle school, the boys will have picked up the pace, and many will be

So how's the weather up there?

your height or even taller. In the meantime, stand up straight, look these boys in the eye, and say, "The weather's just fine, thanks."

Trying to Be Brave

Dear *Help!*,

I have a sickness called epilepsy. I was diagnosed a few days ago. I guess you could say I'm a little ashamed about it. I know I shouldn't be, but I am. I've got so much on my mind! My parents think I'm being brave about it, but I'm not. Sometimes when I'm alone in my room I just break down and cry.

Ashamed

Of course you cry! Any girl would! It's scary to be told you have to live with a disease, and lonely in a terrible way. But being brave doesn't mean locking up your feelings. Let your parents know you're sad and scared. Ask them to hold you! It's also important to learn about epilepsy. Write down every question you have, including things like "Should I tell my friends?" and "What if I get sick at school?" Show the list to your parents and your doctor and get some answers. You'll soon begin to see epilepsy for what it is—a medical condition. *There is nothing shameful about it*. Two million Americans have epilepsy, and most lead very normal lives. Tell yourself that you will, too.

Trying to Be Nice

Dear *Help!,*

I have this girl in my class. She shows off a lot and she cries a lot. A lot of people tease her. I have a lot of friends. I don't want her to be my friend, I just want to help her be a regular girl. How can I help her?

Rita

By showing your friends and classmates how to forgive this girl for her mistakes. Don't make a big deal out of it when she shows off. Don't roll your eyes or make a face if she cries. Don't gossip about her. Most of all, when you hear other kids talk about her as if she had no feelings, remind them that she does. When you see them teasing her, speak up and say it's mean. If you can make even a handful of kids more tolerant, this girl may be able to relax and feel more like a regular girl—and more able to act like one, too.

Uninvited Guest

Dear *Help!*,

I have a good friend who always calls and invites herself over, even if I don't want her to. What should I do?

Erin

Option 1: The next time this girl calls and says, "Can I come over?" say, "No. This isn't a good day." Don't get drawn into talking about reasons she can't come. Keep saying no politely and firmly till she accepts it.

Option 2: Ask your mom to help. It may be easier for her to tell this girl what she needs to hear: "We like having you here, but let us invite you. Please don't invite yourself."

Unloved

Dear *Help!*,

I have a problem. Here it is: I feel like my family doesn't love me any-more. I'm always getting into trouble, getting yelled at or sent to my room. I can't stop being naughty. I don't want this unloved feeling anymore.

Your parents are angry and frustrated, and when you look at them you see it in their eyes. The miserable feeling this gives you may be one reason you're finding it hard to stop being naughty. So write your mom and dad a letter that says you're really lonely and miss feeling close to them. Ask each one to spend some time with you in the next week, just to talk and have fun. Also, ask yourself if something's going wrong at school or with your friends. Sometimes bad feelings can leak from one part of your life into another. If you can fix the other problem, you may find it easier to stay out of trouble at home, too. If none of these ideas work, talk to the counselor at school. Helping kids is her job. Give her a chance to help you.

Worrywart

Dear *Help!*,

I am worrying about the stupidest things lately. I'm turning into a worry-wart! The worst thing of all is that I'm turning into the kind of people who write in to you with all those problems. I really don't want to turn into one of those people. What should I do?

Not wanna be like them

When worry is steaming up the windows of your brain, throw them open. Talk to people—your parents, your sister, your brother, your good friend, anyone you like and trust. What do they think? What would they do? Asking for advice doesn't mean you're a wimp. It doesn't mean you can't solve your own problems. It means you're resourceful. You can learn a lot from other people. Best of all, when worries are brought into the open air, many of them dry up and blow away.

the real YOU

Dear *Help!*,

My friend tells me that more people will like me if I look for the real person I am inside me. I don't know who that real person inside me really is, but I want people to like me. What should I do? I like the way I am now!

Worried in Vermont

If your behavior is causing you problems with other kids, work to change it. But don't twist yourself up like a pretzel looking for some mysterious other "you." Instead, pay attention to your feelings. Be honest, with yourself and with others.

Listen to other people but think for yourself. Never do something to make people like you if it's going to end up making you like yourself less. Now check out the mirror. Is there any doubt whose face is staring back?

Zilch

Dear *Help!*,

I'm going into middle school. Last year I was the best—a queen, everything. Next year, I'll be nothing, nada, zippo, zilch. HELP!

Rebecca

Well, you've got a point. Older kids tend to set the styles and call the tune in any school. But get out a photograph of yourself from kindergarten. Think—*really* think—about how far you've come since then. How many times have you been new and green and felt you couldn't do it? And how many times did you find that you could? You're a capable girl! Besides, you're not going to middle school alone. A lot of your classmates are going, too. You can figure it all out together— talking, playing, laughing, learning as you always have. Being top dog at your old school gave you a lot of confidence. Make up your mind you're going to take that confidence with you.

Even More Help!

A big problem can make you feel as if you're looking at the world from the bottom of a hole. You feel cut off from other people—even from those who love you best. Help seems a million miles away.

It's not. You don't have to face your problems alone. If you haven't found the advice you need in this book, look to the people you trust. Talk to your parents, grandparents, neighbors, friends. Talk to teachers and counselors at school.

These people can't solve a problem for you, but they can help in a big way. They can listen to you when your heart is sad. They can suggest solutions when you think you've tried them all. They can hook you up with people in the community whose job it is to help kids like you.

Gather up all the advice and ideas you can find. Try one thing, then another—and keep at it till you find something that works.